Mnemonics; New Theories and Laws for Memorizing, and Their Practical Application to the Cultivation of the Memory

MNEMONICS

NEW THEORIES AND LAWS FOR MEMORIZING, AND
THEIR PRACTICAL APPLICATION TO THE
CULTIVATION OF THE MEMORY

BY

KIKUJIRO WADAMORI

AUTHOR OF "WADAMORI'S THEORIES AND LAWS OF MNEMONICS," BY WHICH THE
SYSTEM HAS BEEN INTRODUCED INTO SEVERAL UNIVERSITIES AND COLLEGES
IN JAPAN, AND OF "THE PRACTICAL APPLICATION OF MNEMONICS
TO THE JAPANESE CIVIL AND CRIMINAL CODE," ETC.

PRINTED FOR THE AUTHOR
BY
J. B. LIPPINCOTT COMPANY, PHILADELPHIA

PREFACE.

THE study of this system of mnemonics, established for economizing time and labor, gives every one of us a wonderful and mysterious power by which we can easily memorize anything if seen or heard only once, even when so difficult that we could never otherwise memorize it. What is this wonderful and mysterious power that can be obtained by studying this system? From the results given by my many students, I can state definitely that it is, for instance, as follows:

1. Memorizing about one hundred simple words seen or heard only once, such as "nightingale, ink, sea, nail, sun, book, willow, earth, fish, star, etc., etc." (Chapter I., Part II.)

2. Memorizing about one hundred numbers seen or heard only once, such as "3, 5, 9, 2, 0, 6, 8, 3, 5, 8, 9, 1, 0, 4, 9, 2, 7, 5, 6, 0, etc., etc." (Chapter I., Part III.)

3. Memorizing about fifty letters taken in disorder, seen or heard only once, such as "G, H, I, W, E, Z, O, X, T, N, C, S, P, I, S, L, Q, W, H, B, etc., etc." (Chapter III., Part I., and Chapter I., Part II.)

4. Memorizing about thirty foreign words seen or heard only once, such as "Yama (mountain), umi (bow), gakumon (study), shomotsu (book), kami (paper), te (hand), kao (face), hana (flower), koshikake (chair), niwa (garden), etc , etc." (Chapter II., Part III)

Is it possible for any one using only common sense to learn

this system of mnemonics and to apply it without any difficulty? Yes! he can learn it without difficulty and apply it as easily and effectually as I, the inventor, have succeeded in doing. I presume that the most of my readers stand in the same position that I once stood in, wondering what can be done to strengthen the memory and quicken the formation of impressions on the brain. But when they shall have understood that they have the mysterious faculty of memory, created within them and in their fellow-creatures as well, and that to facilitate the use of this mysterious power of memory there are certain rules especially useful and suitable which were formerly hidden, but which were discovered by myself, they will scarcely have the word "wonder" or "impossible" on their lips. Indeed, the study and application of mnemonics are by no means impossible to any one, because they are nothing but the process of adopting practically the mysterious power of memory by using several other powers in the brain. For this reason mnemonics can be easily applied to things and facts from the moment its rules and methods are understood. In this respect the application of the system may be different from that of other arts and sciences, which generally require long and tedious practice. This statement might appear too bold were its truth not proven by the following facts:

First. I have various testimonials in my hands, given by those Japanese students whom I have instructed on the science of memory. In these testimonials they conjointly declare that, to their great surprise, they were able to apply the rules and methods of mnemonics as soon as they understood them. They also declare that there is nothing that cannot easily be memorized by this scientific method.

Second. Even I, as the inventor of this system of mnemonics, had at first some doubt about the result of my own practical tests every time something looked difficult which I desired to memorize; still, that doubt was always overcome by my process—that is, I was always able to memorize everything without any difficulty whenever I properly applied the scientific rules and methods. That many persons have often been surprised at the results of my practical tests is simply due to my application of mnemonics. In short, our mysterious power of memory is capable of immeasurably valuable results, if the rules and methods of the science are properly employed. From my long experience I am sure that those who shall have read through this book will entirely confirm the statement I have made above, and will be able to estimate my work at its true value.

KIKUJIRO WADAMORI.

TOKIO, JAPAN.

CONTENTS.

PART I.
General Discussion.

CHAPTER I
DEFINITION OF MNEMONICS AND ITS GENERAL PRINCIPLES AND RULES

SEC.		PAGE
1	Definition of Mnemonics	13
2.	Principles	14
3.	Rules	18

CHAPTER II.
MEMORY OBJECTS.

1.	Things and Facts or Events	19
2.	Words	20
	A Simple Words	20
	B Connected Words	20
	C Disconnected Words	21

CHAPTER III.
FUNDAMENTAL PROCESSES AND METHODS.

1.	Transformation	23
	A Literal Transformation	24
	B Transformation by Identical Sound	25
	C Transformation by Analogous Sound	25
	D. Dividing Transformation	27
	E. Representing Transformation	27
	F. Composing Transformation	28

CONTENTS.

SEC.		PAGE
2 Association		31
A Modes of Association		32
I Denoting Mode		32
II Composing Mode		37
III Attributing Mode		37
IV. Imagining Mode		37
B. Precedent Word and Subsequent Word		38
C. Order of the Words taken to Form an Association of Ideas		38
D Form of Associating Ideas		39
3. Methods		40
I. Registering Method		40
II Linking Method		40
III. Composing Method		40

PART II.
General Application of Methods.

CHAPTER I.
REGISTERING METHOD.

1. Explanation of the Method		42
A Establishment of the Registering Method		42
B Construction of Mental Register		43
I. Conditions Required for the Mental Register		43
II. Form of the Mental Register and Its Construction		44
III Repetition of the Register		51
2 Application of the Method		52
A. Simple Words		53
B. Connected Words		59
C. Disconnected Words		60

CHAPTER II.
LINKING METHOD.

1. Explanation of the Method		61
2 Application of the Method		63
A. Simple Words		63

CONTENTS.

SEC.		PAGE
B	Connected Words	64
C	Disconnected Words	65
	I Relation of Disconnected Words to Linking Method	65
	II. Classes of Disconnected Words	65
	III. Examples for Memorizing Disconnected Words	67
3	Linking and Registering Methods	72

CHAPTER III.
COMPOSING METHOD.

1.	Explanation of the Method	78
2.	Application of the Method	79
	A Simple Words	79
	B Connected Words	80
	C Disconnected Words	80
3	Difference between the Linking and the Composing Methods	82
4	Difference between the Registering and the Composing Methods	83
5.	Combined Application of the Methods	84

PART III.
Application of the Methods in Regard to Special Objects.

CHAPTER I
MEMORIZING NUMERALS.

1	Transformation of Numerals	90
	A. Transformation of the Digits	90
	B Transformation of the Numerals in Two Order	92
	C Transformation of the Numerals in Three Order	96
	D. Transformation of the Numerals consisting of the Same Numeral Characters in More than Two Order	102
	E. Transformation of the Numerals consisting of the Zeros in More than Two Order	104
	F. Transformation of the Numerals in Four or More Order	104
2.	Transformation of Numerical Words denoting the Numeration	108
	A. Transformation of Numeration into Letters	108

SEC.		PAGE
B	Origin of the Representing Characters of Numeration.	109
C.	Transformation of Representing Characters of Numeration into Adjectives.	109
D	Simple Words which Consist of Combining the Representatives of the Numerations and Those of the Numerals . .	110
E	Transformation of Numerals denoting the Orders	113
3. Exercise of Memorizing Numerals		116
A	Memorizing Numerals by Registering Method	117
B.	Memorizing Numerals by Linking Method	118
C	Memorizing Numerals by Combined Application of Registering, Linking, and Composing Methods	119

CHAPTER II.

MEMORIZING FOREIGN LANGUAGES

1. Special Rules for the Transformation 123
2 Transformation and Association 127
3 Analysis of Transformation and Association 131
4. Application of the Several Methods to the Foreign Languages. . 131

CHAPTER III

MEMORIZING SENTENCES AND SPEECHES.

1. Rules 134
2 Exercises 134

CHAPTER IV

MEMORIZING POETICAL COMPOSITION

1. Rules 142
2 Exercises 142

CHAPTER V.

MEMORIZING NAMES (PERSONAL).

1. Rules 147
2 Exercises 148

CONTENTS. 11

CHAPTER VI.

Memorizing Unfamiliar or Unknown Things and Events or Facts and Connection of the Names with Them.

SEC		PAGE
1	Kinds of Things and Events Unknown	150
2	Special Rules for Transformation.	150
	I. Representation by Selection	150
	II Representation by Identification	151
	III Representation by Analogy	151
	IV Representation by Position	151
	V. Representation by Attributing	151
3	Transformation of Unknown Things or Facts into Words	152
	A Transformation of Unknown Persons into Words	152
	I Transformation of Unknown Persons in Whom Special Features Can be Found	152
	II Transformation of Unknown Persons in Whom Special Features Cannot be Found	153
	B. Transformation of Unknown Birds, Quadrupeds, Insects, and Fish into Words	158
	C Transformation of Unknown Grasses, Trees, Metals, Stones, and Tools into Words	159
	D Transformation of Unknown Stars, Mountains, Rivers, Cities, Villages, and Islands into Words	159
	E. Transformation of Unknown Events or Facts into Words	160
4.	Application of the Registering Method for Memorizing Unknown Things and Events Transformed into Words	160
5.	Memorizing Connections of Unknown Things and Events or Facts with Their Names	162
	a Rules	162
	b Exercises	163

CHAPTER VII

Application of Mnemonics to the Study of Sciences

1. Geography 165
2. History 167
3. Law 168
4. Physics, Chemistry, the Medical Science, etc. 169

APPENDIX.

		PAGE
I	The Time and Method Required for Studying this Science	171
II	The Permanence of the Memory	172
III.	Forgetfulness	173
IV	The Benefit of Mnemonics	174

COMMENDATORY EXPRESSIONS 181

MNEMONICS.

PART I.

GENERAL DISCUSSION.

CHAPTER I.

DEFINITION OF MNEMONICS AND ITS GENERAL PRINCIPLES AND RULES.

§ 1.—Definition of Mnemonics.

FOR convenience in the consideration of the subject of Memory we make a division of it into two classes,—"Natural or Uncultivated Memory" and "Scientifically Cultivated Memory." The difference between these two gives rise to the science of "Mnemonics," or "Mnemotechny." This difference is, therefore, the main topic of this chapter.

I. Natural or Uncultivated Memory is that capacity or ability of an individual to receive, retain, and recall impressions received from the outside through the sense organs, and impressions formed in the mind itself, *without* the aid of scientific methods.

II. Scientifically Cultivated Memory is that capacity or ability of an individual to receive, retain, and recall impressions received from the outside through the sense organs, and impressions formed in the mind itself, *with* the aid of scientific methods.

It can now be readily understood that the Natural or Uncultivated Memory depends entirely upon the natural retentive power of the brain, and that the Scientifically Cultivated Memory is simply the Natural Memory reinforced by the application of systematic and scientific methods, which transform and associate the various impressions by the several mental acts, considering, imagining, analyzing, etc.

There is another difference between the Uncultivated and Cultivated Memory, depending upon the ability to recall impressions already received and retained. In the case of a Natural Memory the power to recall impressions depends alone upon the natural or unaided reproductive power of the brain, while the Cultivated Memory is dependent upon the natural power, reinforced and aided by attempted recollection of the systematic methods by which the impressions were received and retained, which makes it possible to recall, at almost the same moment, the impression itself.

We can now arrive at a satisfactory definition of mnemonics. *Mnemonics* is the science which treats of the practical application of systematic acts and methods bearing upon the Cultivation of a Natural or Uncultivated Memory.

§ 2.—Principles.

There are nine fundamental principles to be studied in relation to mental acts and ideas. We shall consider them one by one, giving such examples as are necessary to bring out the meaning and use of each.

FIRST PRINCIPLE —The mind has naturally the power to construct a new impression by exchanging one impression for another which has some relation to the original impression, and also the power to recall both impressions by means of recalling either one of them.

Example.

The number "29" is suggested, and we wish to exchange this idea for another one. We may let the letter "t" represent "2" and the letter "n" represent "9". To combine these letters we may make use of the letter "i" as an auxiliary letter. Thus, "tin," forming a new idea. We now have two impressions, i. e., "29" and "tin," and the simple recollection of either one will recall the other by the association of ideas.

SECOND PRINCIPLE.—The mind has naturally the power to construct one or more ideas and arrange them in order as the links in a chain, and also the power to recall all the impressions by recalling any one of them.

Example.

We receive the two simple impressions, "book" and "snow." We may combine them into one complex impression, thus "A book is found in the snow." When any one of these three ideas is recalled—two are simple ideas and one is complex—we can recall the rest by association of ideas. Again, we may receive these four simple impressions, "book, snow, hat, and mail." We may combine these four simple ideas into three complex ideas. "A *book* has a cover white as *snow;*" "*snow* covered one's *hat*;" "a *hat* is worn by the *mail* carrier." When one of the four simple impressions is first recalled, or when one of the three complex impressions is first recalled, the rest will be recalled by the association of ideas.

THIRD PRINCIPLE.—The mind has naturally the power to construct an idea by combining many ideas with one main idea (which may be chosen to suit the individual's taste), and also the power to recall all the impressions by first recalling any one of them.

Example.

The following six simple impressions are received, "moon, train, tiger, clock, mountain, and lead-pencil," and to memorize them more easily we may connect them into one complex idea. Now we may choose any idea as a main idea which will virtually stand for the whole. For example, we will combine these six simple ideas into the following complex idea, and choose as the main idea the expression "travelling by train" (or any other expression may be chosen). For instance, make the complex idea thus: "In the moonlight the swiftly moving train frightened a large tiger, and as the clock struck twelve a mountain came into view, and I wrote its name with a lead-pencil." We have now six simple ideas and one complex idea, and when any one of them is recalled or when the main idea (travelling by train) is recalled, the rest are recalled by the association of ideas.

FOURTH PRINCIPLE.—The mind has naturally the power to retain familiar ideas or impressions more firmly than novel or unfamiliar ones.

Explanation.—By a familiar idea we understand that a considerable time has elapsed since the idea or impression was received and retained in the mind. It is also a natural supposition that it has not only been recollected several times, but that it has also been applied practically, and is therefore a fixed impression.

The firmness or weakness of the memory depends entirely upon the degree to which an idea has been impressed upon the mind. The oftener we recall an idea the firmer we stamp it into the mind; for example: suppose that the first recollection makes an impression the depth of which is represented by the tenth of an inch; each time we recall the idea afterwards we increase the depth by a fraction of an inch, and it finally becomes a lasting impression.

But novel ideas make less of an impression because they have not met with recollection or application. Hence, as novel ideas do not make as deep an impression on the memory as familiar ones, they cannot be expected to be retained as long.

FIFTH PRINCIPLE.—An individual has naturally the power to memorize a comprehended idea more easily than an uncomprehended one.

SIXTH PRINCIPLE.—An individual has naturally the power to memorize connected ideas more easily than disconnected ideas.

Explanation.—These two last-mentioned principles are based upon the same facts. As pleasure or pain are to the senses, so are the comprehended and uncomprehended ideas, the connected and disconnected ideas, to the brain in reference to the classification of ideas

The brain is so constructed as to more easily retain the comprehended ideas and connected ideas than the uncomprehended and unconnected ideas When we read a book or hear a lecture, if the meaning is made clear by connected words and sentences we find no difficulty in remembering the whole subject without any special effort, while if the contrary is the case, and the words and sentences are not connected, we find it almost impossible to memorize the subject.

Examples

1 "Daniel Defoe, the author of 'Robinson Crusoe,' was born in London" This complex idea is a connected idea, and undoubtedly a comprehended one, and can be memorized after hearing or reading it once But if we interchange the words, forming a complex idea of this kind, i e , " Was born, in, the author of, London, Daniel Defoe, 'Robinson Crusoe,'" we have a disconnected and uncomprehended idea which would be very difficult to memorize at once, as it is composed of words arranged regardless of their meaning or relation to one another

2 "19, 17, 15, 13, 11, 9, 7, 5, 3, 1 " This row of ten figures is a comprehended idea because they are odd numbers in sequence, placed in reverse order This comprehended idea can easily be memorized after seeing or hearing it once But should these figures be arranged without regard for their natural order, thus, "17, 9, 15, 19, 13, 3, 7, 1, 11, 5," we will have an uncomprehended idea as well as a disconnected one, which consequently cannot be easily memorized

Figures and words when arranged regardless of order are difficult to memorize because they form ideas which, as they are unconnected and uncomprehended, are disagreeable to the sense.

SEVENTH PRINCIPLE.—The mind has naturally the power to retain more easily ideas which affect the sensibilities than ideas which do not affect them.

Explanation —We know when we meet with an extraordinary circumstance it is strongly impressed on the mind because it affects the sensibilities, but an ordinary occurrence does not affect us, so we do not so readily remember it Hence there are different degrees, according to the effect upon the sensibilities

EIGHTH PRINCIPLE.—The individual has naturally the power to memorize a simple idea more easily and firmly than a complex one.

Explanation —A simple idea makes a clearer and stronger impression on the mind than a complex one, and consequently is more easily retained.

NINTH PRINCIPLE.—The mind has naturally the power to memorize an original idea more easily and firmly than an acquired one.

Explanation —1 An original idea is formed by the brain itself, but an acquired idea is formed by the impressions received into the brain through the senses, and is not so closely related to the individual.

2 An original idea is generally formed by the brain as a result of impressions already existing in the mind, while an acquired idea is often made up of unfamiliar ideas

3 An original idea is readily formed by the brain, but an acquired one is more difficult

The above points explain why an original idea is more durable than an acquired idea, and why it makes a deeper impression.

§ 3.—Rules.

From the nine fundamental principles just explained the following rules are deduced:

RULE I. All *acquired ideas* should be exchanged for *original ideas*. (Principles 1, 2, 3, and 9.)

RULE II. All *unfamiliar ideas* should be associated with *familiar ones*. (Principles 1, 2, and 4.)

RULE III. All *uncomprehended ideas* should be exchanged for *comprehended ideas*. (Principles 1, 2, 3, and 5.)

RULE IV. All *disconnected ideas* should be exchanged for *connected ideas*. (Principles 1, 2, 3, and 6.)

Rule V. All *unaffecting ideas* should be exchanged as often as possible for *affecting ideas.* (Principles 1, 2, 3, and 7.)

Rule VI. All *complex ideas* should be exchanged as often as possible for *simple ideas.* (Principles 1, 2, 3, and 6.)

CHAPTER II.

MEMORY OBJECTS.

The objects of memory are various and innumerable. For convenience in the application of the several rules we classify them into several kinds. This chapter, then, deals with this classification, which is made according to the nature of the object, and is first divided into two main groups,— "Things and Facts or Events" and "Words." We will now consider the first group.

§ 1.—Things and Facts or Events.

"Things and facts or events" are subdivided into two classes, namely, "familiar things and facts or events" and "unfamiliar things and facts or events," which are each subdivided into simple and complex.

The first subdivision, "familiar things and facts or events," is closely allied to the "words" which represent the "things and facts or events;" that is to say, the presence of "things and facts or events" recalls the "words" which correspond to them, and the presence of the "words" recalls the things and events which correspond to the "words." Hence, the rules which apply to the one will apply to the other; and since such is the case, we have not devoted any special space to the consideration of "familiar things and facts or events," as this class is covered in the discussion of "words." But in memorizing "unfamiliar things and facts or events" of which the names are unknown, the case is quite different from the former, and the advantage of memorizing them by words is not present.

The difference between "familiar" and "unfamiliar things and facts or events" requires a special discussion.

To avoid the confusion which might arise in treating the two classes of objects in the same place, a special place will be set aside in Part III. for the discussion of "unfamiliar things and facts or events."

§ 2.—Words.

Words are divided into two kinds,—familiar words and unfamiliar words. Again, familiar words are separated into three classes, namely: *A*, simple words; *B*, connected words; and *C*, disconnected words. Unfamiliar words have no subdivision, and they are, for the convenience of the application of the method, always treated as disconnected words in this Mnemonics, because most of the unfamiliar words always bring us disconnected words in their transformation.

A. Simple Words.—A simple word is a single word, such as a noun, pronoun, verb, adjective, etc., including alphabetical characters and certain numbers.

N B —The following ten numbers, "0, 1, 2, 3, 4, 5, 6, 7, 8, 9," and each of the numbers from 10 to 99, which will be explained under "The Transformation of Numerals" (Part III), and certain foreign words, which are also explained in the chapter on "Memorizing Foreign Languages," are also treated as simple words

B. Connected Words.—Connected words are two or more words joined together into phrases, clauses, or sentences. Those words which are so connected must have such a formation that they can be committed to memory by means of one of the words which should represent the whole, so that when recalling that which was committed we shall be able to recall the whole by recalling the representative word described above.

Example.

1 Familiar sayings: "Open season," "to have a bee in one's bonnet;" "to rain cats and dogs," "to eat one's words," "bells, bells, oh! silver bells;" "union forever!" "long live the queen!" "a rolling stone gathers no moss;" "the schoolmaster is abroad," "beauty is but skin deep," "a burnt child dreads the fire;" "the pen is mightier than the sword"

2 Familiar names and addresses. George Washington; Napoleon Bonaparte; Queen Victoria; City Hall, Broad and Market Streets, Philadelphia, Pennsylvania

3 Certain numerals which are explained in a special chapter

N B —To facilitate the application of this science, the relation of simple words to simple things and facts or events will be explained as follows · Simple things and facts or events cannot always be represented by simple words, therefore they must sometimes be represented by connecting two or more words, as for a complex thing; for instance red rose, fountain pen, United States, or "University of Pennsylvania," which is represented by three connected words, and for events as follows Civil War, Japan-China War In the next chapter, on the association of ideas, simple words, things, and facts or events are treated equally under the head of "ideas" In forming an associated idea, a simple word or a simple thing or fact or event is used as the unit

If a connected word denotes only a simple object, and if that object is regarded as a unit in forming an association of ideas, a connected word performs the same function as a simple word.

C. Disconnected Words.—A disconnected word is one which consists of two or more simple words or groups of connected words which have no connection with or relation to one another.

Explanation.—A disconnected word differs from a connected word in having no relation or connection with the several simple or connected words which compose it, so that neither the commitment of one of them to memory helps to memorize the rest, nor the recollection of one of them helps to recall the rest

Examples.

1 Disconnected words may consist either of nouns or verbs, i e , "book, table, flower, pen, picture, mountain, women," or "sleeping, singing, running, walking, riding." Together they form a disconnected word, as the examples already given, "open season," "to have a bee in one's bonnet," "to rain cats and dogs," etc , these when taken singly are connected words, but when taken together are disconnected words.

2 Unfamiliar names and addresses form disconnected words, i e., Toyotomi Hideyoshi, No 619 Owari Street, Nagoya, Aichi, Japan.

3 Numerals composed of more than three figures form disconnected words, i e , "4,629," "53,052," "915,372 "

4 All the unfamiliar foreign words which do not belong to the classes of simple or connected words are disconnected, i e , "gakumon" (Japanese, study), "Gedachtniss" (German, memory), "soleil" (French, sun)

N B —These words are simple words in their original language, but they are regarded as disconnected words in this system of mnemonics, as already explained

CHAPTER III.

FUNDAMENTAL PROCESSES AND METHODS.

THE fundamental process of mnemonics is an act of the mind by which all memory objects are brought into and retained in the mind. It answers all the requirements of the six rules. According to the critical investigation of the author there are two such processes, namely : I. Transformation ; II. Association. Although the process of Association was established long ago, the process of Transformation is entirely new, and the author may be credited with the establishment of it. In the opinion of the author, no other fundamental process can be discovered besides these two.

FUNDAMENTAL PROCESSES AND METHODS. 23

The application separately of the two processes to all objects of memory is found to be impossible, because memory objects are so complicated and varied that in order to meet such cases means are sought in the latter part of this chapter which consist of the combined application of the two processes regulated by certain fixed methods. This complication gives rise to three methods, the explanation of which will be given in the latter part of the chapter.

§ 1.—Transformation.

Transformation is the process of changing given words which are difficult to memorize or associate into other words which may be easily memorized or associated. There are six different ways of transforming.

Explanation.—We learn by experience that in memorizing some ideas in their original form, we find it is very difficult to retain them,—for instance, dates in history, botanical names, names of places, etc. The object of the process of transformation is to lighten the labor of memorizing these things and to enable us to easily and accurately remember any idea we wish by transforming the original idea into a new idea, but at the same time retaining certain relation to the original idea, so that when we recall the transformed idea we can remember the original one

Examples.

1 The number twenty-nine (29) is not easy to memorize in its present form, but as we have already seen in the "First Principle" in Chapter I , we can memorize it easily by changing it to "tin "

2 The letters "c" and "r" are memorized in a similar manner by using "a" for the auxiliary letter, forming the word "car " In an attempt to associate several ideas it often happens that some ideas are found that are impossible to associate into one idea The process of transformation is applied to such cases If we have two given ideas we change one of them or both for other closely related ideas and associate them, i e , "29" and "vase " We transform "29" to "tin," as described before, and, bringing the transformed idea with a remaining given idea, we have "tin vase " Now "29" and "vase" can be easily remembered by the idea "tin vase " Therefore the transformation of ideas is a preparatory process to the association of ideas

A. LITERAL TRANSFORMATION.

Literal Transformation is the process by which we facilitate memorizing ideas or forming associated ideas by constructing a new word out of the words required to be memorized or associated. This is done by adding to or removing from the word a letter or letters, or by changing one or more letters of the word. Hence there are three natural subdivisions of Literal Transformation, *i.e.*, *a*, adding; *b*, removing; and *c*, changing, transformation.

1. Adding Transformation.

This is the process of forming a new word by adding a letter or syllable or another short word to the construction of the original.

Examples of Adding Transformation

1 let—inlet.	5 ton—tongue	8 ear—earth.
2 on—son.	6 kit—kitten.	9 hand—handsome.
3 land—island	7. sun—sunk	10 nail—snail
4 wine—twine.		

2. Removing Transformation.

This is the process of forming a new word by removing a letter or letters, syllable, or another short word from the original word. Examples may be obtained by reversing the process described under "Adding Transformation," *i.e.*, inlet—let, etc.

3. Changing Transformation.

This is the process of forming a new word by changing a letter or letters in the original word.

Examples of Changing Transformation

1 let—set	5 wine—wind	8. ear—car.
2. on—ox	6 cat—cut	9 hill—mill
3 hand—land	7. sun—sin	10. hum—hem.
4 ton—son		

B. TRANSFORMATION BY IDENTICAL SOUND.

This is the process of facilitating the association of an idea by exchanging the given word for another word having an identical sound, but a different meaning.

Examples of Transforming by Identical Sound.

1 rain—reign.
2 no—know.
3 bee—be
4 ant—aunt
5. nun—none
6. son—sun
7. sees—seize.
8 right—write
9 beet—beat
10 fir—fur

C. TRANSFORMATION BY ANALOGOUS SOUND.

This is the process of facilitating the association of ideas by exchanging a given word for another word which is similar in sound, but different in meaning. This process is similar to literal transformation, but the difference is explained thus,—literal transformation depends upon the spelling of the words, while transformation by analogous sound depends upon the sound of the words, not the spelling.

Analogous sounds are divided into two classes: Class 1, depending upon method of making or forming the sounds; Class 2, depending upon the length of sounds.

Examples

CLASS 1.—DEPENDING UPON METHOD OF FORMING SOUNDS.

a. Letters

a, e, i, o, u, have analogous sounds.
b, f, p, v, have analogous sounds
c, g, j, s, z, have analogous sounds
d, t, th, have analogous sounds
k, g, c, q, have analogous sounds
l, r, have analogous sounds
m, n, have analogous sounds

MNEMONICS.

b Words

pen, pin, pan,   have analogous sounds.
cup, cap,   have analogous sounds.
cod, god,   have analogous sounds.
coat, goat,   have analogous sounds.
bet, bat, bit,   have analogous sounds.
sink, zinc,   have analogous sounds.
quest, guest,   have analogous sounds.

The length of the sound of a word depends upon the length of the vowels which compose it. As we have explained that there is an analogy of sound between the five vowels, there is not much need of further explanation, but as there is a great chance for confusion, we shall consider this subject for the purpose of showing that there is a difference, and an important one.

CLASS 2.—DEPENDING UPON THE LENGTH OF THE SOUND.

a Letters

ā is analogous to ă.
ē is analogous to ĕ.
ā is analogous to ī.
ē is analogous to ĭ.
ō is analogous to ŏ.
ōō is analogous to ŏŏ.
ū is analogous to ŭ.

b. Words

taste is analogous to test.
bean is analogous to bin.
code is analogous to cod.
kill is analogous to keel.
sell is analogous to sail.
tail is analogous to tell.

D. DIVIDING TRANSFORMATION.

Dividing transformation is the process of dividing a given word into two or more syllables or words for the purpose of associating ideas.

Examples

Given word	moonlight,	railroad,	incomprehensibility
Transformed word	moon light,	rail road,	in com pre hen si bility
	island,	Brookline	
	is land,	Brook line	

N B.—1 In this transformation the lines drawn under the syllables or parts of the words denote the several parts of the words to be divided

2 The object of this transformation is to form familiar words from unfamiliar or meaningless ones But it will be noticed that there still remain some meaningless ones in the transformation, but these syllables are again transformed into words by adding letters to them, so that the transformation in this case is really a preparatory process for the formation of familiar words This method is generally applied for memorizing all the disconnected words

E. REPRESENTING TRANSFORMATION.

Representing Transformation is the process of representing the whole of the words to be memorized by a part of them or by entirely new words which have some relation to the original idea.

Representing Transformation is divided into three classes, *i.e.*,—

1 Transformation by selected word
2 Transformation by selected letter
3 Transformation by selected different word

1. Transformation by Selected Word.

This is the process of selecting one or more words from the words to be memorized to represent the whole.

N B.—It makes no difference what part of the words to be memorized is selected for representing the rest

Any word may be selected from the whole to suit the taste of the individual

Examples.

a. Given words—Kingdom of Great Britain.
   Transformed word—Britain
b Given words—Money is power.
   Transformed word—Money.
c Given words—A burnt child dreads the fire
   Transformed word—Fire

2. Transformation by Selected Letter.

This is the process of selecting one or more letters or characters from the words to be remembered to represent the rest. This process is most useful in transforming numerals.

Examples.

"T" is selected from two
"F" is selected from four
"S" is selected from six
"G" is selected from eight

3. Transformation by Different Word.

This is the process of representing words to be remembered by selecting an entirely different word closely related to the original in meaning.

Examples.

a Given words—The United States of America
   Transformed word—Jonathan
b. Given words—A rolling stone gathers no moss.
   Transformed word—Tussor
c. Given words—Kikujiro Wadamori
   Transformed word—Mnemonics

F. COMPOSING TRANSFORMATION.

This is the process of composing a simple word with two or more letters or with two or more simple words, or of composing a connected word with two or more simple words.
This transformation is divided into two classes, *i e.,*—

a Composition of a simple word
b Composition of a connected word.

FUNDAMENTAL PROCESSES AND METHODS. 29

Examples of Class a.
1. "o" + "x" = "ox"   4. "p" + "in" = "pin"
2. "co" + "d" = "cod"   5. "ax" + "le" = "axle"
3. "ki" + "te" = "kite"   6. "con" + "tempt" = "contempt."

Examples of Class b.
1. "poor" + "man" = "poor man"
2. "sun" + "shine" = "sunshine"
3. "travelling" + "in" + "the moonlight" = "travelling in the moonlight"
4. "bird" + "flying" + "in the sky" = "bird flying in the sky"

THE COMBINED APPLICATION OF THE SEVERAL TRANSFORMATIONS,

When we desire to transform several words we find that it is necessary to use all the transformations combined. It is important that a careful study should be made of the combined application of these six transformations, and it will be necessary for the study of mnemonics to practise the following examples until no difficulty remains in forming them.

Examples.

(a) The number "89," or "eighty-nine," is transformed into a new word by the combined application of three different transformations, i e, *first* the numerical words "eighty-nine" are transformed into two letters, "g" and "n," by means of "Transformation by Selected Letters," *second*, a letter, "u," is added to one of the letters by "Adding Transformation," making the new syllable "gu," *third*, "gu" and "n" are formed into a new word, "gun," by "Composing Transformation," and the process of transformation is completed

(b) The word "then" is transformed into the word "thunder" by the combined application of two transformations,—i e, *first*, "then" is transformed into "thun" by changing transformation; *second*, the syllable "der" is added to "thun" by adding transformation, and we have formed a new word, "thunder," and the process of transformation is completed

(c) The word "Japan" is transformed into a connected word, "jam pan," by the combined application of three transformations,—i e, *first*, the word "Japan" is transformed into the syllable "Jap" and the word "an" by dividing transformation, *second*, the letter "p" of "Jap" is changed to "m," forming "jam" by changing transformation, and "an" is made into "pan" by adding transformation; *third*, the transformed words "jam" and "pan" are composed into a connected word, "jam pan," by composing transformation, and the transformation is completed.

(*d*) The word "Atlantic" is transformed into three words, "bat," "run," "tick," by the combined application of three transformations,— *i.e.*, *first*, the word "Atlantic" is divided into the word "at" and the two syllables "lan" and "tic" by dividing transformation; *second*, the letter "b" is prefixed to the word "at," and forms the new word, "bat," by adding transformation; *third*, the syllable "lan" is transformed into "run" by transformation by analogous sounds; *fourth*, the syllable "tic" is transformed into the new word "tick" by adding transformation (the same as in the second step), and the transformation is completed.

(*e*) The letters "h" and "w" are transformed into a connected word, "hardware," by the combined application of two transformations,— *first*, "h" and "w" are transformed into simple words, "hard" and "ware," by adding transformation; and, *second*, "hard" and "ware" are composed for "hardware."

(*f*) The letters "l," "g," and "u" are transformed into a connected word, "large gun," by the combined application of the three transformations,—*first*, "l" is transformed into "large" and "g" and "u" into "gun;" *second*, "large" and "gun" are transformed into "large gun."

TRANSFORMATION:
- I. Literal Transformation:
  1. Adding Transformation.
  2. Removing "
  3. Changing "
- II. Transformation by Identical Sounds.
- III. Transformation by Analogous Sounds:
  1. Depending upon method of forming the sound.
  2. Depending upon the length of the sound.
- IV. Dividing Transformation.
- V. Representing Transformation:
  1. By selected word.
  2. By selected letter.
  3. By different word.
- VI. Composing Transformation:
  1. Composition of simple words.
  2. Composition of connected words.

§ 2.—Association.

Association is the process of forming a new complex idea (association of ideas) by combining two given ideas. There are four different methods of associating ideas. In many cases of associating two ideas we often find it difficult to discover a relation between them, even if one of them or both of them have been already transformed as just described. Hence, the process of associating ideas explains the several modes, which are established by examining all the possible relations which could exist between the two words or ideas; and, also, there are explained laws which facilitate the accurate formation of association. If this process is applied carefully with the process of transformation there is no reason why many things which are required to be memorized should not be remembered without difficulty. The explanation of the present subject is classified in the following table:

ASSOCIATION.
- A. MODES OF ASSOCIATION
  - I. Denoting Mode
  - II. Composing Mode
  - III. Attributing Mode.
  - IV. Imagining Mode
    - 1. Identity.
    - 2. Identical sound
    - 3. Analogy
    - 4. Analogous sound.
    - 5. Contrary
    - 6. Causation
    - 7. Specification
    - 8. Accompaniment
    - 9. Locality
    - 10. Time
    - 11. Contiguity
    - 12. Demonstrating
- B. PRECEDENT AND SUBSEQUENT WORDS
- C. ORDER OF THE WORDS TAKEN TO FORM AN ASSOCIATION OF IDEAS
- D. FORM OF ASSOCIATING IDEAS.

A. MODES OF ASSOCIATION.

The purpose of the modes of association is to form an association between two ideas by defining the several relations which exist between them. There are four modes of association, *i.e.*, denoting, composing, attributing, imagining.

I. DENOTING MODE

Denoting mode is to associate two ideas into a new complex idea by denoting a relation constantly existing between them or by explaining a fact about them. This mode is subdivided into twelve classes.

1. Identity.

This is to associate two ideas into a new idea by denoting that they are identical in every respect or some respect; although they differ in meaning they are identical in construction, and although different in nature they are identical in one or more of their shapes, characters, or uses.

Explanation —There are many different cases in this mode 1. "Apple" is identical with "apple" in every respect, as the two words represent the same object 2. "Japan" is identical with "Chrysanthemum Empire" in every respect but a difference of construction, for they both represent the same object. 3. "Kerosene oil" and "candle" are identical only in respect to use (lighting), and different in substance, construction, and meaning. 4. "Umbrella" is identical with "mushroom" in that they look somewhat alike, but they differ in every other respect

Examples for Associating these Ideas.

1 "Apple" and "apple" are the same thing 2 "Japan" and "Chrysanthemum Empire" are identical in meaning 3 "Kerosene oil" and "candle" are identical in use 4 "Umbrella" and "mushroom" are identical only in appearance

2. Identical Sound.

The explanation and examples of "Association by Identical Sound" are the same as those given under the "Trans-

FUNDAMENTAL PROCESSES AND METHODS.   33

formation by Identical Sound." The application of this mode is as follows: "reign" to "rain," or "know" to "no," are identical in sound.

N.B.—This mode must really be included in the last, but, as it is extremely useful in practice, we have especially established it as a "mode of association"

3. Analogy.

This mode is the process of associating two ideas into a new idea by denoting that a resemblance exists between them in respect to meaning or quality.

Examples for Analogy Mode.

1 "Forest" and "wood" 2. "Opera house" and "theatre" 3. "Incandescent light" and "arc light" 4. "Bad" and "wicked."

4 Analogous Sound.

Explanation and examples of this mode are the same as for "Transformation by Analogous Sound" (*vide ut supra*). The method of forming an association of ideas by this mode can be understood from the preceding mode.

This mode was established for the same reason that the "identical sound" was established beside "identity."

5. Contrary.

This mode is the process of associating two ideas into a new idea by denoting that they are contrary or opposite in quality or meaning.

Examples for Contrary Mode

1 "Eastern Hemisphere" and "Western Hemisphere" 2 "South Pole" and "North Pole" 3 "Palace" and "hut" 4 "Day" and "night" They are associated thus "Day and night are just contrary"

6. Causation.

This mode is the process of associating two ideas into a new idea by denoting that they are related in cause and effect.

Examples for Causation Mode

1. "Study" and "knowledge." 2 "Sickness" and "death" 3 "Sun" and "day" 4 "Cloud" and "rain." They are associated thus: "Study is the cause of knowledge," or, "Death is the effect of the sickness"

7. Specification.

This mode is the process of associating two ideas into a new idea by denoting that they are related by genus or species.

Examples for Specification Mode.

1 "Animal" and "dog" 2 "Salmon" and "fish" 3 "Flower" and "rose" 4. "House" and "brick house" They are associated thus: "Animal includes dog," or, "Salmon belongs to fish"

8. Accompaniment.

This mode is the process of associating two ideas into a new idea by denoting that one is accompanied by the other in use.

Examples for Accompaniment Mode

1 "Scientist" and "books" 2 "Musician" and "musical instruments" 3 "Fish" and "water" 4 "Store" and "goods" In these cases a scientist is always accompanied by books, a musician by instruments, etc.

9. Locality.

This mode is the process of associating two ideas into a new idea by denoting that both of them are in the same locality, or, if one of them is a locality the other one is included in it. There are two cases in this mode:

1 Two ideas having a relation to the same locality
2 One idea having a relation to one locality, $i\,e$, the other idea

FUNDAMENTAL PROCESSES AND METHODS. 35

In the first illustration New York and Massachusetts are associated by denoting that they are both in the United States.

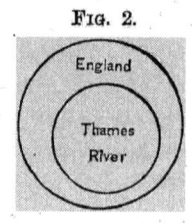

FIG. 1.　　　　　　　　FIG. 2.

In the second illustration we associate Thames River and England by denoting that the former exists in the latter.

Examples for Locality Mode.

1. "North America" and "United States." 2. "Washington" and "United States." 3. "Pyramids" and "obelisks." 4. "China" and "India." In these cases, North America and United States are associated by denoting that the latter exists in the former, and pyramids and obelisks are associated by denoting that they both exist in Egypt.

10. Time.

This mode is the process of associating two ideas into a new idea by denoting that both of them exist in the same time or season, or when one of them is a time or season the other exists in it. There are two classes in this mode, i.e.:

1. Ideas which happen or exist in the same time.
2. An idea which happens or exists in a time,—i.e., the other idea.

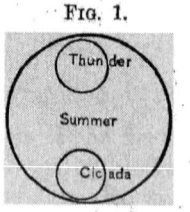

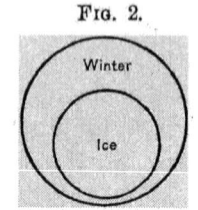

FIG. 1.　　　　　　　　FIG. 2.

In the first illustration we associate thunder and cicada by denoting that they both exist in the summer. In the other illustration we associate by denoting that ice exists in winter.

Examples for Time Mode

1 "Snowing" and "sleighing" 2 'Spring" and "flowers" 3 "Night" and "sleeping" 4 "Sunday school" and "Sabbath school" These examples are associated as follows "Snowing and sleighing both exist in winter," "Flowers exist in the spring," etc.

11. Contiguity.

This mode is the process of associating two ideas into a new idea by denoting that they are approximate to each other in position or order.

Explanation —There are four classes to this mode; *i e.:*

    a Relating to locality
    b. Relating to position or direction.
    c Relating to order of existence.

Examples for Contiguity Mode

    a Relating to locality.

1. "France" and "Germany." 2 "Asia" and "Europe"

    b Relating to position or direction.

1. "Top" and "side" 2 "North" and "East"

    c Relating to the order of existence

1 "A" and "B" 2 "July" and "August."

They are associated thus "France and Germany are approximate," or, "A and B are approximate in their alphabetical positions"

12. Demonstration.

This mode is the process of associating two ideas into a new idea by showing that a positive fact or unalterable truth exists concerning them.

Examples for Demonstration Mode.

1 "Exercise" and "study" 2 "War of succession" and "railroad" 3 "Sword" and "gunpowder" 4 "Sick man" and "medicine"

They are associated thus "Exercise is necessary for studying people," or, "Sword and gunpowder are used for war"

II. COMPOSING MODE.

For the definition and examples of this mode the reader is referred to the article under "Composing Transformation" (*vide ut supra*); for instance, "o" and "x" = ox, etc.

III. ATTRIBUTING MODE.

This mode is the process of associating two ideas into a new idea by attributing (limiting or qualifying) one by the other.

Examples for Attributing Mode.

1 To associate two ideas, "scenery" and "Hudson River," we form the new idea : "The scenery of the Hudson River" 2 To associate the two ideas "men" and 'walk" = "walking men" 3 To associate the ideas "hundred" and "soldiers" = "a hundred soldiers" In these cases the ideas "scenery," "men," and "soldiers" are limited or qualified by the other ideas, "Hudson River," "walking," and "hundred"

IV. IMAGINING MODE.

This mode is the process of associating two ideas into a new idea by imagining certain facts in regard to them ; *i e.*, when there is no apparent relation between two ideas we may associate them by supposing some fact about them. It is not necessary that this supposition should be a probable or possible fact, but, on the contrary, the more impossible it is the more easily it can be memorized, as it will make an impression as a "novel idea." For instance, to associate the ideas "snow" and "book" we may suppose this to be the case "As I was sitting by the window reading, the *snow* came in and wet my *book*."

Examples for Imagining Mode

1 "London" and "dragon" 2 "Himalayas" and "America" 3. "Pacific" and "Fuji Mountain" 4 "Snow" and "desert." 5. "Niagara' and "Washington."

Association —1. "I went to London to see a dragon." 2. "From the top of the Himalayas I expected to see America." 3. "Many people cross the Pacific to climb Fuji Mountain." 4. "Did you ever see snow covering the desert?" 5. "Washington could not have crossed Niagara in a boat."

B. PRECEDENT AND SUBSEQUENT WORDS.

As two ideas or words are always associated together in this Mnemonics, it is convenient to give them some definite name, therefore we will give to the first of the two words or ideas the name "precedent word" and to the second the name "subsequent word."

C. ORDER OF THE WORDS TAKEN TO FORM ASSOCIATION OF IDEAS.

It is obvious that those things heard, seen, or considered must be recalled in the same order as they were memorized. If, therefore, in the formation of an associated idea we transpose the object in the first position to the second position we may be misled in the recollection by considering the object as originally in the second position, and our memory will become imperfect by erring in the order of ideas. For this reason the following rules have been established pertaining to the order of words in forming association of ideas.

a. Proper Order of Words.

This order is placing the precedent word first and the subsequent word second (in relation to one another).

b. Exceptional Order of Words.

This order is placing the subsequent word first and the precedent word second, in the reverse manner of the preceding rule. In our experience it is often impossible to use the proper order and form a properly associated idea; then the exceptional order is necessary to form a clear idea. This exceptional order, while it may be confusing at first, will with practice become very simple and useful.

D. FORM OF ASSOCIATING IDEAS.

There are three ways of forming association of ideas,—affirmative, negative, and expressive forms.

a. Affirmative Form.

This is the form of associating two ideas by affirming a fact concerning the precedent and the subsequent word.

Examples.

1 *London* is part of *England*   2 The highest mountains in *North America* are the *Rocky Mountains*.   3. *Flowers* are *beautiful*.   4 *Mnemonics* is the best friend of *students*

N.B.—The italicized words are the ones to be associated

b. Negative Form.

This is the form of associating two ideas by disaffirming a fact concerning the precedent and the subsequent words.

Examples

1. *Coral* is not a *plant*   2 All *animals* are not *human beings*   3. *Human beings* cannot *fly*.   4 *War* is not *pleasure*

c. Expressive Form.

This is the form of associating two ideas by expressing some fact concerning them without affirmation or negation.

Examples.

1 A *large garden*   2 Writing a *letter* in the *moonlight*   3 The *beauty* of *flowers*   4 *Excellent scenery*

N B.—As it has been proven by the author that affirmative ideas make firmer impressions than negative or expressive ideas, it is better for the reader to use affirmative forms as much as possible.

§ 3.—Methods.

These methods consist of combining the application of the two fundamental processes (*i. e.*, transformation and association) practically and systematically to the many cases fulfilling the requirements of the six rules. There are three methods in this system of mnemonics.

It is believed that the relation between the fundamental processes and methods of mnemonics is identical with the relation of addition, subtraction, multiplication, and division to the methods in arithmetic. If one of the four fundamental processes is disregarded in the methods of arithmetic, no doubt the use of arithmetic loses a great deal of its importance. And the same is true in mnemonics.

We have established three methods for the combined application of the two fundamental processes, as follows: registering, linking, and composing methods.

I. REGISTERING METHOD, which consists of registering new ideas by associating with familiar ideas already memorized (from Rules I., II., and V.).

II. LINKING METHOD, which consists of linking several new ideas together in order or sequence. (Rules I., III., IV., and V.)

III. COMPOSING METHOD, which consists of composing or forming many ideas into one main idea. (Rules I., III., IV., and V.)

N B —1. These methods are more fully explained in Part II.

2 In the application of the registering method the words already memorized or registered are the *precedent* words, and the new words which are to be memorized are the *subsequent* In the application of the linking and composing methods the first word to be memorized is the precedent word and the rest are the subsequent words in the first association, and in the second association the second word to be memorized is the precedent word and the third the subsequent word.

3. It must be remembered that all words are associated in pairs in the system of mnemonics, thus making it necessary, if there are more than two ideas, to make several associations.

4. In the application of the registering method, associations must be formed for every word to be memorized, so if there are ten simple words, ten associations must be found. In the linking and composing methods the association will be less by one than the words to be memorized; if there are ten simple words to be memorized, nine associations will be required. In regard to the relation between the number of associations and the number of ideas to be memorized, the connected word is the same as the simple in every respect; and disconnected words transformed into connected and simple words are just the same individually as a connected or simple word.

PART II.

GENERAL APPLICATION OF METHODS.

CHAPTER I.

REGISTERING METHOD.

§ 1.—Explanation of the Method.

THE registering method, as already explained, is the method of recording memory objects into the "mental register" by means of a "mental pen" which represents the several mental acts. We will first consider the reason for the establishment of this method and then take up the construction of the "mental register."

A. ESTABLISHMENT OF REGISTERING METHOD.

The memory objects of which impressions are received into the brain through the senses, and the thoughts and imaginations formed in the brain itself, are numberless.

As many people do not know how to memorize, and depend upon recording such objects as are to be memorized upon paper, which may become lost or destroyed, and as this is in many other ways a very unsatisfactory method, it can be seen that any method which will develop that power which every animal has (*i.e*, natural memory) will aid us in acquiring a much more satisfactory and infinitely more reliable method of retaining impressions. Consequently the author has spent a great deal of time in the consideration of the construction of what he calls a mental register, in contradistinction to a material register (such as paper and books), and the method of registering is called "registering method."

This registering method is to associate with the "mental register" every external and internal impression that may be required to be memorized by acts of the several mental powers,—imagination, consideration, and judgment,—which are collectively called the "mental pen." Hence there are three important factors in this registering method, *i.e.*, "mental register," "mental pen," and "mental registration."

1. The Mental Register is the knowledge or experience of every individual, *i.e.*, it is all the things, facts, and words arranged in regular order in our brain.

2. The Mental Pen, as already described, is the mental actions,—imagining, considering, and judging, etc.

3. The Mental Registration is to form an association of ideas by means of the "mental pen" between the "mental register" and the objects to be memorized, according to the rules of transformation and association.

B. CONSTRUCTION OF MENTAL REGISTER.

I. CONDITIONS REQUIRED FOR THE MENTAL REGISTER.

In a material register, consider the thickness of the paper, its quality, and size; if the paper is thick and hard, it may be preserved for a long time; if it is of good quality, the same is true, and if it is of large size, many things can easily be recorded on it. If the register is well arranged, one can easily examine it and search for any required entry.

This is all true of the mental register. As already stated, recording in the mental register with the mental pen is to associate the objects required to be memorized with the mental register. Hence the objects or words composing the mental register must be of such a character that the mental pen is able to act upon it quickly and easily. Therefore if each object or word used as a mental register is comprehensive enough in meaning, it is not difficult to form with them any thought or imagination, and, also, it is not difficult to form an association of ideas. And if the objects or words forming the mental register be those that are easily remembered and are arranged in regular order, so that no two words are alike in the same register, the associations formed are most clearly and firmly impressed, and consequently can be preserved a longer time. Again, if the objects or words composing the register are uniformly arranged and subdivided, it is very easy to recollect the order of association formed, just as a register furnished with an index and arranged with all the recorded matter classified is easy of access.

If we neglect one of the above conditions we will not have a perfect register. Hence a perfect mental register consists of three factors:

1. Words or objects widely applicable in meaning.

2. Words or objects that are clearly remembered and have a regular arrangement and there is no repetition.

3. Words or objects that have fixed number and arrangement.

II FORM OF MENTAL REGISTER AND ITS CONSTRUCTION.

(A.) PROPER REGISTER.

A proper register is one which contains all the conditions necessary to form a perfect register.

We will now consider the objects or words necessary to form a proper register.

a. Matter or Things.

Such facts as action, intercourse, war, walking, etc., or such things as county, country, city, house, mountain, river, glass, tree, bird, beast, insect, fish, etc., may have the first condition, but not the second and the third, and thus are insufficient to be a proper register.

b. Signs of Matters and Things.

In the signs of matters and things, that is, word and letter, there are three kinds. Some may be proper registers and some may not. These are words, letters, and numbers.

1. Words.

Some nouns, adjectives, verbs, and adverbs are susceptible of several meanings, and therefore comprehensive enough to satisfy the first condition of a proper register. An article, a pronoun, a conjunction, a demonstrative adjective, a preposition, and an interjection are generally poor in meaning, but they can be easily transformed into the former kinds of words by means of the several transformations. All these words, therefore, are good in the first condition, and consequently every sentence is good as it consists of these words. But almost all English sentences make a repeated use of articles and prepositions, and therefore there are few sentences which will satisfy the second condition except some short maxims and phrases to which every English ear is accustomed. But they have no special arrangement, therefore there can be no perfect register of words in the English language. Some part of a sentence may satisfy the second condition as follows: thus,—

1 "They tell us, sir, that we are weak,—unable to cope with so formidable an adversary."

46   MNEMONICS.

  2 "But, alas! you are not all here. Time and the sword have thinned your ranks"
  3 "'Tis some visitor," I muttered, "tapping at my chamber door,
      Only this and nothing more"

But if every syllable and word in a poem of insufficient meaning, used as a proper register, be transformed into a word which has a sufficient meaning by several transformations, they will all be adopted as the proper register; for example—

GIVEN WORDS.

"Bring the good old bugle, boys! we will sing another song,
  Sing it with a spirit that will start the world along,
  Sing it as we used to sing it, fifty thousand strong,
  While we were marching through Georgia"

TRANSFORMED WORDS

Bring *theatre* good old bugle, boys! *wedding* will sing *ancient athlete err son*,
  Singe itch wither ape spire pit thatch willow start *theft* world *arm long;*
  Sink Italian ass web used *tong zinc kit fife type thought sand* strong,
  Wild weed war march inn throw georgic giant.

Explanation of the Transformation.

1. "Oth," the second syllable of the word "another," was first transformed into a syllable, "ath," by the transformation by analogous sound; secondly, into a word, "athlete"

2. "Sing," first word in third line, was transformed into "sink" by the changing transformation

3. "While" was transformed into "wild," removing the letters "h" and "e" forming it by the removing transformation, and adding the letter "d" to it by the adding transformation

4. "Were," "ing," and "through" were transformed into "war," "inn," and "throw" by the transformation by analogous sound

5. "All the transformed words besides were transformed by the adding transformation.

We now have a large proper register consisting of a poem transformed. This register has forty words and four lines; each line from the first to the third has thirteen words and the last line eight. It is sure that twenty or thirty songs at least are known by everybody throughout the country. Therefore, if they adopt transformed songs as the register, a great many proper registers will be easily prepared for them.

2. Letters.

The alphabet is too simple to satisfy the first condition, but for satisfying the second and third conditions its letters are the best examples. If, therefore, we transformed them as in the preceding example of the poem, they form a most perfect register. For instance, "A" may be transformed into "ale," "B" into "bee," "C" into "cat," "D" into "day," etc. Hence we have a perfect register numbering twenty-six words, as follows:

A—ale	J—jar	S—sun.
B—bee	K—kite.	T—toy
C—cat	L—lamb	U—uncle
D—day	M—moon.	V—valley.
E—egg	N—nuts	W—wax.
F—fly	O—ox	X—xebec.
G—gun	P—pin.	Y—yard.
H—horse	Q—quail	Z—zinc.
I—ice.	R—rain	

If we want a larger register, we may omit the vowels from the alphabet, and by connecting them to each of the twenty-one consonants we will get a register numbering one hundred and five, as follows:

B—ba, bat; be, beggar, bi, bite; bo, bone; bu, bull
C—ca, cat; ce, ceiling; ci, cider, co, comb; cu, cucumber
D—da, day; de, den; di, dike; do, dog; du, dummy.
F—fa, face, fe, fence, fi, fight, fo, fox, fu, fur.
G—ga, gamble, ge, gentlemen, gi, giant; go, goat, gu, gun
H—ha, ham, he, hem, hi, hill; ho, honey; hu, human
J—ja, jar, je, jelly; ji, jill, jo, joy, ju, just
K—ka, kangaroo, ke, keel; ki, kite; ko, Koran; ku, kummel.

L—la, lard; le, leg, li, life, lo, love; lu, lump
M—ma, man; me, means, mi, mine, mo, moon, mu, much
N—na, name; ne, net; ni, night; no, noise, nu, number.
P—pa, pan; pe, pen, pi, pin, po, pond, pu, pupil
Q—qua, quail, que, question; qui, quill; quo, quorum, quu, quota
R—ra, rat; re, remain, ri, ring, ro, roof; ru, ruin
S—sa, sale, se, seal; si, sigh, so, song, su, sun
T—ta, tail, te, teeth; ti, tide; to, tomb, tu, tube
V—va, vase; ve, velvet; vi, victim; vo, voyage; vu, vulture
W—wa, wax, we, wedding; wi, wife, wo, wolf; wu, woman
X—exa, example; exe, exempt, exi, exist; exo, exonerate, exu, exult
Y—ya, yarn, ye, yellow, yi, yield; yo, yoke; yu, yule
Z—za, zambo, ze, zeal; zi, zinc, zo, zone; zu, zuche

There are two cases where no word can be applied; these are "quu," "wu." In these cases the preceding vowels will be again applied; that is, instead of "quu" we use "quo, quota," instead of "wu" we use "wo, woman," and so on. "Q" must always be used in connection with "u." "X" will be used with "e" preceding it, as in "example." For convenience "X" and "Z" can be taken away from the register of consonants because they are very difficult to connect with some vowels, and then nineteen consonants will remain as the register. Besides these, if we adopt "ch, sh, th, and kn," etc, as consonants, the register will be enlarged. They will follow "Z" in alphabetical order as follows:

Ch—cha, charm, che, chest, chi, child; cho, choke, chu, church
Ph—pha, pharmacy, phe, pheasant, phi, philanthropy, pho, photograph, phu, phonograph *
Kn—kna, knapsack; kne knell; kni, knife; kno, knowledge; knu, knuckle.
Th—tha, thanks; the, theme; thi, thief; tho, thought; thu, thunder.
Wr—wra, wrap, wre, wreck; wri, wrinkle; wro, wrong, wru, wrung

---

* *Vide supra.* This combination cannot be used, so we use preceding vowel again

REGISTERING METHOD. 49

If we want a still larger register, connect the vowels before each consonant as follows:

B—ab, absent, eb, ebb, ib, ibex; ob, obstacle, ub, ubiquity.
C—ac, account, ec, ecclesiastic, ic, icicle; oc, occasion; uc, ocean,* etc

N B —"Ch, ph, kn, th, wr, st, and stv" cannot be adopted as consonants in the present case because we are unable to connect the preceding vowels with them In the above examples there are sixteen cases where no word can be formed unless the vowel be changed

These again make a register numbering one hundred and five words, and if used in connection with the preceding one, we will have a register numbering two hundred and ten words.

3. Numerals.

Numerals equally with the alphabet have not a comprehensive meaning in their original state, and thus are deficient in the first condition. But for the second and third conditions there is no better register than these. It is not impossible to make them satisfy the first condition, as in the case of the alphabet. As the method to do so is very confusing, we will consider it under a different part,—that is, the chapter for memorizing numerals.

(B.) COMMON REGISTER.

The common register is one that satisfies one or two of the conditions required for the proper register. Thus, matters and words that can be adapted as the common register are very numerous. It may properly be said that all the objects and words in one's memory are included in this class.

---

* *Vide supra* This combination cannot be used, so we use preceding vowel again

a. Matters and Things.

1. ACTUAL FACTS.—For instance, all the important events experienced by one's self formerly or during the last year, or during the time from the first day of this year up to the present day, or acts and events during a day,—that is, things done or met with during the time from the getting up to the nightly repose, or those facts heard or seen in the theatre or at some other entertainment. If those facts are remembered in right order, they can well serve for a common register.

2. ACTUAL THINGS.—All the parts of one's body or of one's house or well-known places, that is, village, county, state, country to which they belong. These things will serve for the common register. (Mnemonics as commonly taught is of this nature.) But in the present case there is not any necessity for adopting these facts and things as a common register, for it is far more convenient to adapt the word representing them than the things and facts themselves.

b. Words.

1. All the words representing the actual facts and things described in the preceding are common register.

2. A man's address—for instance, "Mr. James Washington, No. 9 Canal Street, Ithaca City, Cayuga County, New York State"—makes a common register numbering fourteen words.

3. Famous maxims, proverbs, and phrases to which ears are accustomed.

(C) DIFFERENCE BETWEEN THE USE OF THE PROPER REGISTER AND THE COMMON REGISTER.

1. The proper register is the most useful for memorizing numerous objects which are divided into several classes.

The common register is best adapted to matters small in number and without classification.

2. By means of the proper register we can instantly recollect the order or position of each object memorized as it is required, but memory by the common register makes it very hard to do so.

3. Until one is well trained in the formation of associations it is better to use the proper register, and the common register may be adopted after his training has been well developed.

4. The association formed by the proper register is clear and certain, while that by the common register may be confused and uncertain; but this difficulty can be avoided after the training has been improved.

5. A new common register can be made at any time as it is wanted, but the proper register cannot be easily made, and therefore it is necessary to prepare it beforehand.

6. In view of the adaptation of the registering method to daily business and scientific study there is not much difference between the two kinds of register. To the students who want to memorize large books, it may sometimes be more convenient to use a number of the common registers at one time.

III REPETITION OF THE REGISTER.

The mental register, either proper or common, may be used repeatedly without any disadvantage. For instance, when one wants to associate twenty ideas to this register, "there are many rare abilities in the world that fortune never brings to light." Although each object is associated with each word there still remain six objects to be associated. In this case one can again use the same register and associate the remaining objects with the first six words in the same register. It is better, however, not to repeat a register for the same mass of matter. If it is adopted for a different mass of matter at a different time there is no confusion or uncertainty in the formation of the associations, no matter how many times it may be repeated. So far the mental register is superior to the actual register, for the actual register cannot be used more than once; if it is used again the first and second records cannot be clearly distinguished; and, again, the mental register lasts as long as the brain, for nothing but some terrible disease or death can destroy it, however often it may be used.

MENTAL REGISTER :
- I Mental Register
  - a Proper register
    - 1 Words
    - 2 Transformed letters
    - 3 Transformed numbers.
  - b Common register.
    - 1 Actual matter.
      - a Facts
      - b Things.
    - 2 Signs of matter: { Words
- II Mental Pen.
  - a Consideration
  - b Imagination
  - c Judgment
- III Mental Registration
  - Forming association of ideas according to the several rules

§ 2.—Application of the Method.

This exercise is to enable us to associate the matters to be memorized into the register in the right order; that is, first object with the first word in the register, second with the second, and so on. The objects and register should be examined first according to the rules relating to association and transformation when an association is to be formed between them.

A. SIMPLE WORDS.
Example 1.
I. Proper Register
Alphabet.

A, B, C, D, E, F, G, H, I, J, K, L, M, N, O, P, Q, R, S, T, U, V, W, X, Y, Z

TRANSFORMED WORDS

1	Ape	10	Journey	19	Senator
2	Bee.	11	Kitten	20	Tin.
3	Ceiling	12	Lily.	21	Uncle
4.	Deer	13	Man	22	Vehicle.
5	Eagle	14	Northern	23	Waterloo
6	Fire	15	Old	24	Export
7	Georgia	16	Pupil	25	Yellow.
8	Head	17	Quail	26	Zinc
9.	Ice	18	Restless		

II. Words to be Memorized

1	Minister	10	Japan.	19.	Assemble.
2	Doctor	11	Cry	20	He
3	Leaves	12	Beautiful	21	Sing
4	Bear.	13	Prowess.	22	Disease.
5	Tree	14.	Indian Ocean	23	Napoleon
6	Country	15.	Children	24	Hong Kong
7.	America.	16	Foreign language	25	Soup
8	Helmet	17.	Yes	26	Brooklyn Bridge.
9	Fish	18	And		

III Registration.

1 *Apes* are disliked by the *minister.*
2. The *bee* stung the *doctor*
3 The *ceiling* is ornamented with a design of *leaves*
4 The *deer* is not as strong as a *bear*
5 An *eagle* dwells in the branch of a large *tree.*
6. Large *fires* are rare in the *country*
7 *Georgia* is in North *America*
8 The *head* is protected by a *helmet*
9 *Iced fish*
10 A *journey* to *Japan*
11 The *kitten cries*
12 The *lily* is *beautiful*
13 A *man* must have *prowess.*

MNEMONICS.

14. The *Northern Sea* and *Indian Ocean* have different climates.
15. The *old* man is very kind to *children*.
16. The *pupil* learns a *foreign language*.
17. I shot a *quail yesterday*.
18. The *restless ants*.
19. The *senators assembled* to-day.
20. *Tin* melts in the *heat*.
21. My *uncle sings*.
22. A *vehicle* to convey *diseased people*.
23. *Waterloo* was a hard blow to *Napoleon*.
24. The *export* from *Hong Kong*.
25. *Yellow*-colored *soup*.
26. I picked a piece of *zinc* on the *Brooklyn Bridge*.

IV. ANALYSIS OF REGISTERED IDEAS.

No. of Ideas.	Association.			Transformation.	
	Mode.	Order.	Form.	Precedent word.	Subsequent word.
1	Imagining.	Proper.	Affirmative.	Adding.	None.
2	Attributing.	Proper.	Expressive.	Adding.	None.
3	Imagining.	Proper.	Affirmative.	Adding.	None.
4	Denoting.	Proper.	Negative.	Adding.	None.
5	Denoting.	Proper.	Affirmative.	Adding.	None.
6	Denoting.	Proper.	Affirmative.	Adding.	None.
7	Denoting.	Proper.	Affirmative.	Adding.	Composing.
8	Attributing.	Proper.	Expressive.	Adding.	None.
9	Composing.	Proper.	Expressive.	Adding.	None.
10	Attributing.	Proper.	Expressive.	Adding.	None.
11	Imagining.	Proper.	Affirmative.	Adding.	None.
12	Denoting.	Proper.	Affirmative.	Adding.	None.
13	Denoting.	Proper.	Expressive.	Adding.	None.
14	Denoting.	Proper.	Affirmative.	Adding.	None.
15	Denoting.	Proper.	Affirmative.	Adding.	None.
16	Imagining.	Proper.	Affirmative.	Adding.	None.
17	Imagining.	Proper.	Affirmative.	Adding.	Adding.
18	Attributing.	Proper.	Expressive.	Adding.	Changing.
19	Imagining.	Proper.	Affirmative.	Adding.	None.
20	Denoting.	Proper.	Affirmative.	Adding.	None.
21	Imagining.	Proper.	Affirmative.	Adding.	None.
22	Attributing.	Proper.	Expressive.	Adding.	None.
23	Denoting.	Proper.	Affirmative.	Adding.	None.
24	Attributing.	Proper.	Expressive.	Adding.	None.
25	Attributing.	Proper.	Expressive.	Adding.	Composing.
26	Imagining.	Proper.	Affirmative.	Adding.	None.

V. Explanation of the Applications of the Table.

1 "A" is transformed into "ape" by adding transformation. The precedent word "ape" and the subsequent word "minister" are associated by imagining that "apes are disliked by the minister" This association is made by taking the words in proper order and affirming a fact.

2 "B" is transformed into the "bee" by adding transformation The precedent word is associated with the subsequent word "doctor" by expressing a truth, "The bee stung the doctor" This association makes use of the words in their proper order and expresses a truth

3 "C" is transformed into "ceiling" by adding transformation The precedent word "ceiling" and the subsequent word "leaves" are associated by imagining that "the ceiling is ornamented with a design of leaves" This association makes use of words in proper order and affirms a fact.

4 "D" is transformed into "deer" by adding transformation The precedent word "deer" and the subsequent word "bear" are associated by denoting a truth, "that the deer is not as strong as a bear" This association takes the words in their proper order and negatives the truth.

5 "E" is transformed into "eagle" by adding transformation The subsequent word "tree" is transformed into "large tree" by composing transformation. The precedent "eagle" and the subsequent words "large tree" are associated by explaining a truth that "an eagle dwells in the branches of a large tree" This association takes the words in their proper order and affirms the truth

6. "F" is transformed into "fire" by adding transformation, and again into "large fire" by composing transformation The precedent "large fire" is associated with the subsequent "country" by explaining the truth that "large fires are rare in the country" This association takes the words in their proper order and affirms a truth.

N.B —We believe that these explanations will make the table clear to all.

MNEMONICS.

Example 2.

I Proper Register.

1. Ba	6 Ca	11 Da
2 Be.	7 Ce	12 De
3 Bi	8 Ci	13 Di.
4 Bo.	9 Co	14. Do
5. Bu	10 Cu	15 Du

II. Words Required to be Memorized.

1 Minister	6 Country	11 Cries.
2 Doctor.	7. America	12. Beautiful.
3. Leaves	8 Helmet	13. Prowess
4. Bear.	9 Fish	14 Indian Ocean.
5 Tree.	10 Japan.	15. Children

III. Registration

1. (Ba—minister) The *baby* of the *minister*.
2. (Be—doctor) The *best doctor*
3. (Bi—leaves) A man *bid* for some *leaves*.
4 (Bo—bear) The *bones* of a *bear*.
5 (Bu—tree) A *bushy* branch of a *tree*
6. (Ca—country) A *cat* ran to the *country*
7 (Ce—America) *Central America*
8 (Ci—helmet) A *circus* exhibited an ancient *helmet*.
9 (Co—fish) *Cod* belongs to the *fish* family
10 (Cu—Japan) *Customs* of *Japan*
11 (Da—cries) The *daughter cries*.
12 (De—beautiful) *Deer's* fur is *beautiful*
13. (Di—prowess) A man of *dignity* has *prowess*
14 (Do—Indian Ocean) A *dock* on the shore of the *Indian Ocean*.
15 (Du—children) *Dutch children*

IV. Analysis of Registered Ideas.

No. of Ideas.	Association.			Transformation.	
	Mode.	Order.	Form.	Precedent word.	Subsequent word.
1........	Attributing.	Proper.	Expressive.	Adding.	None.
2........	Attributing.	Proper.	Expressive.	Adding.	None.
3........	Imagining.	Proper.	Affirmative.	Adding.	None.
4........	Attributing.	Proper.	Expressive.	Adding.	None.
5........	Attributing.	Proper.	Expressive.	Adding and composing.	None.
6........	Imagining.	Proper.	Affirmative.	Adding.	None.
7........	Attributing.	Proper.	Expressive.	Adding.	None.
8........	Imagining.	Proper.	Affirmative.	Adding.	Composing.
9........	Denoting.	Proper.	Affirmative.	Adding.	None.
10.......	Attributing.	Proper.	Expressive.	Adding.	None.
11.......	Imagining.	Proper.	Affirmative.	Adding.	None.
12.......	Denoting.	Proper.	Affirmative.	Adding and composing.	None.
13.......	Imagining.	Proper.	Affirmative.	Adding and composing.	None.
14.......	Attributing.	Proper.	Expressive.	Adding.	None.
15.......	Attributing.	Proper.	Expressive.	Adding.	None.

Example 3.

I. Proper Register.

1. Ab.
2. Eb.
3. Ib.
4. Ob.
5. Ub.
6. Ac.
7. Ec.
8. Ic.
9. Oc.
10. Uc.
11. Ad.
12. Ed.
13. Id.
14. Od.
15. Ud.

II. Words Required to be Memorized.

1. Foreign language.
2. Yes.
3. And.
4. Assemble.
5. Be.
6. Sing.
7. Disease.
8. Napoleon.
9. Hong Kong.
10. Soap.
11. Brooklyn Bridge.
12. Minister.
13. Doctor.
14. Leaves.
15. Tree.

III. Registration.

1. (Ab—foreign language) *Able* to speak a *foreign language*.
2. (Eb—yes) I bought some *ebony yesterday*.
3. (Ib—and) The *ibis* is not found in this *land*.
4. (Ob—assemble) The *object* of an *assembly*.
5. (Ub—hero) *Ubiquity* of God is believed by a *hero*.
6. (Ac—sing) *Academy* of *singing*.
7. (Ec—disease) An *economist* contracted a *disease*.
8. (Ic—Napoleon) *Ice* was the strongest enemy of *Napoleon*.
9. (Oc—Hong Kong) I expect an *occasion* to go to *Hong Kong*.
10. (Uc—soap) I know a man in *occupation* of *soap* making.
11. (Ad—Brooklyn Bridge) *Admirable Brooklyn Bridge*.
12. (Ed—minister) An *educated minister*.
13. (Id—doctor) An *idle doctor*.
14. (Od—leaves) The *odious* smell of *leaves*.
15. (Ud—tree) A *udometer* hanging under the *tree*.

IV. Analysis of the Registered Ideas.

No. of Ideas.	Association.			Transformation.	
	Mode.	Order.	Form.	Precedent word.	Subsequent word.
1	Imagining.	Proper.	Affirmative.	Adding and composing.	None.
2	Imagining.	Proper.	Affirmative.	Adding.	Adding.
3	Denoting.	Proper.	Negative.	Adding.	Adding.
4	Attributing.	Proper.	Expressive.	Adding.	Changing.
5	Denoting.	Proper.	Affirmative.	Adding and composing.	Adding.
6	Attributing.	Proper.	Expressive.	Adding.	None.
7	Imagining.	Proper.	Affirmative.	Adding.	None.
8	Denoting.	Proper.	Affirmative.	Adding.	None.
9	Imagining.	Proper.	Affirmative.	Adding.	None.
10	Imagining.	Proper.	Affirmative.	Adding.	None.
11	Attributing.	Proper.	Expressive.	Adding.	None.
12	Attributing.	Proper.	Expressive.	Adding.	None.
13	Attributing.	Proper.	Expressive.	Adding.	None.
14	Attributing.	Proper.	Expressive.	Adding and composing.	None.
15	Attributing.	Proper.	Expressive.	Adding.	Composing.

REGISTERING METHOD.

B. CONNECTED WORDS.

I. Register (Common)

(1) There (2) are (3) many (4) rare (5) abilities (6) in (7) the (8) world (9) that (10) fortune (11) never (12) brings (13) to (14) light.

II Words to be Associated

1. George Washington
2. The pen is mightier than the sword.
3. A rolling stone gathers no moss
4. Bring back my bonnie to me
5. Napoleon Bonaparte
6. Time is money
7. Lord Mansfield
8. Union forever
9. Oxford University
10. Benjamin Franklin
11. A burnt child dreads the fire.
12. Into how many parts is the Wadamorian Mnemonics divided?
13. When first I came to Yale
14. To save a father is a child's chief honor

III. Registration.

1. "There" and "George Washington"—A *theatre* was on *Washington Street*
2. "Are" and "Pen is mightier than the sword."—To make a *pen* is a *useful art*
3. "Money" and "A rolling stone gathers no moss"—*Money rolls* on the bank's desk like *stones* in the road.
4. "Care" and "Bring back my bonnie to me"—*Care* must be taken for one's *bonnie*
5. "Abilities" and "Napoleon Bonaparte"—The *ability* of *Napoleon*
6. "In" and "Time is money"—I spend my *time* reposing in an *inn.*
7. "The" and "Lord Mansfield"—There was a *thief* in a *man's field* last night
8. "World" and "Union forever"—A *union* of all the states in the *world* is a necessity
9. "That" and "Oxford University"—The *hat* of *Oxford students* is of a funny shape.

10. "Fortune" and "Benjamin Franklin"—*Franklin* did not make a *fortune* by his electrical invention.
11. "Never" and "A burnt child dreads the fire"—A *burnt child* was lying near the *river*.
12. "Brings" and "Into how many parts is the Wadamorian Mnemonics divided?"—The *Wadamorian Mnemonics* is more precious than *diamond rings*.
13. "To" and "When first I came to Yale"—*New Haven* has the *tombs* of many scientists.
14. "Light" and "To save a father is a child's chief honor"—My *father* is so *light* that I can carry him on my back.

IV. Analysis of Registered Ideas.

No. of Ideas.	Association.			Transformation.	
	Mode.	Order.	Form.	Precedent word.	Subsequent word.
1...	Imagining.	Proper.	Affirmative.	Changing.	Representing and composing.
2...	Denoting.	Exceptional.	Affirmative.	Composing and changing.	Removing and representing.
3...	Denoting.	Proper.	Affirmative.	Changing.	Removing and representing.
4...	Denoting.	Proper.	Affirmative.	None.	Representing.
5...	Attributing.	Proper.	Expressive.	None.	Representing.
6...	Imagining.	Exceptional.	Affirmative.	Adding.	Representing.
7...	Imagining.	Proper.	Affirmative.	Changing and adding.	Dividing and representing.
8...	Imagining.	Exceptional.	Affirmative.	None.	Representing.
9...	Denoting.	Proper.	Affirmative.	Removing.	Representing and composing.
10...	Denoting.	Exceptional.	Negative.	None.	Representing.
11...	Imagining.	Exceptional.	Affirmative.	Changing.	Representing.
12...	Denoting.	Exceptional.	Affirmative.	Removing.	Representing.
13...	Denoting.	Exceptional.	Affirmative.	Adding.	Representing.
14...	Imagining.	Exceptional.	Negative.	None.	Representing.

C. DISCONNECTED WORDS.

Memorizing disconnected words requires principally the combined application of the linking and composing methods, so it will be explained under these heads.

CHAPTER II.

LINKING METHOD.

§ 1.—Explanation of the Method.

THE linking method is used for forming a consecutive association, like the links of a chain, when it is required to memorize two or more simple, connected, or disconnected words, or to combine the simple or connected words which compose a disconnected word itself.

There are six different cases for the application of the present method, as follows:

1 When it is required to memorize many simple words, the link formed is like the following diagram:

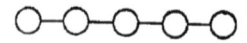

O—O—O—O—O

In this illustration each ring represents a simple word, and the lines denote the association. The relation of a number of words and the association is subject to the note already explained; that is two simple or connected words require one association, and three require two. In the above illustration, therefore, five rings and four lines are required

2 When it is required to memorize many connected words, the link formed is like the following diagram:

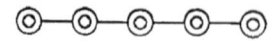

◎—◎—◎—◎—◎

In this illustration each double ring represents a connected word, and the lines the association

3 When it is required to memorize many simple and connected words intermixed, the chain formed is like the following diagram

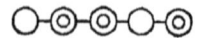

O—◎—◎—O—◎

4. When it is required to memorize a disconnected word, the link formed is like the following diagram:

In this diagram the dotted line represents a disconnected word. The rings and double rings within the dotted lines represent the simple and connected words enclosed in the disconnected word. The lines between them represent the association formed. As is seen, these four associations are likewise formed for one disconnected word.

5. When it is required to memorize many disconnected words, then the link is formed like the following diagram:

As may be seen in the diagram, there are only three disconnected words, while eight associations are required to be formed. Or another link may be formed, as follows.

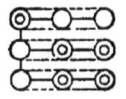

In the preceding diagram it is required, in order to associate several disconnected words with each other, to form associations between the last simple or connected words included in the first disconnected word and the first simple or connected word included in the second successively. But in the present diagram the disconnected words may be associated by forming an association between each first simple or connected word included in the first, second, and third successively, as is shown by the lines.

6. When it is required to memorize simple, connected, and disconnected words intermixed, the diagram is formed as follows:

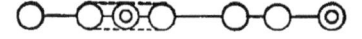

In this diagram there are five words, and the associations formed are six

§ 2.—The Application of the Method.
A. SIMPLE WORDS.

I. Words Required to be Memorized.

1. Tree.
2. Paper.
3. Mountain.
4. Tea.
5. Gladstone.
6. Ocean.
7. Rocky.
8. Engineering.
9. China.
10. Park.
11. Eagle.
12. Beauty.

II. Linking.

1. (Tree and paper) — A small *tree* packed in *paper*.
2. (Paper and mountain) — I have a *paper* on which is drawn a *mountain*.
3. (Mountain and tea) — On the *mountain* there are no *tea* plants.
4. (Tea and Gladstone) — I attended a *tea party* which was held by Mr. *Gladstone*.
5. (Mr. Gladstone and ocean) — The fame of Mr. *Gladstone* is like a *great ocean*.
6. (Ocean and rocky) — The *ocean* cannot be seen from the tops of the *Rocky Mountains*.
7. (Rocky and engineering) — The ascension of the *Rocky Mountains* by train was a great feat of *engineering*.
8. (Engineering and China) — *Engineering* is not developed in *China*.
9. (China and park) — *China* has not many *parks*.
10. (Park and eagle) — I went to the *park* and saw an *eagle*.
11. (Eagle and beauty) — The wings of the *eagle* are *beautiful*.

III. Analysis of Linked Ideas.

No. of Ideas.	Association.			Transformation.	
	Mode.	Order.	Form.	Precedent word.	Subsequent word.
1	Imagining.	Proper.	Affirmative.	Composing.	None.
2	Imagining.	Proper.	Affirmative.	None.	None.
3	Imagining.	Proper.	Negative.	None.	Composing.
4	Imagining.	Proper.	Affirmative.	Composing.	None.
5	Denoting.	Proper.	Affirmative.	None.	Composing.
6	Denoting.	Proper.	Negative.	None.	None.
7	Denoting.	Proper.	Affirmative.	None.	None.
8	Denoting.	Proper.	Negative.	None.	None.
9	Denoting.	Proper.	Negative.	None.	Composing.
10	Imagining.	Proper.	Affirmative.	None.	None.
11	Denoting.	Proper.	Affirmative.	None.	Adding.

B. CONNECTED WORDS.

I Words Required to be Memorized

1. Hear the sledges with their bells! silver bells
2. Strike till the last armed foe expires!
3. Union forever!
4. An innocent man needs no eloquence
5. Sir, the perpetrator of the atrocious crime is a young man
6. Only this and nothing more
7. Work! work! work! till the brain begins to swim.
8. Rome was not built in a day

II Linking

1. ("Hear the sledges with the bells! silver bells" and "Strike till the last armed foe expires!") A gentleman on a *sledge* with *silver bells struck* his *armed foe*
2. ("Strike till the last armed foe expires!" and "Union forever!") After *last armed foe* was *struck* down, a *firm union* of colonies was formed in America
3. ("Union forever!" and "An innocent man needs no eloquence") I saw a man *eloquently* maintaining his *innocence* in the court of the *United States.*
4. ("An innocent man needs no eloquence" and "Sir, the perpetrator of the atrocious crime is a young man") *Eloquence* cannot make a man *innocent* who committed an *atrocious crime.*
5. ("Sir, the perpetrator of the atrocious crime is a young man" and "Only this and nothing more.") *Young man* who is fond of money *only* and *nothing more*
6. ("Only this and nothing more" and "Work! work! work! till the brain begins to swim") *Nothing* is *more* important than *to work* as long as the *brain* will endure.
7. ("Work! work! work! till the brain begins to swim!" and "Rome was not built in a day") The establishment of *Rome* was the *greatest work* of the ancients.

III. ANALYSIS OF LINKED IDEAS.

NO. OF IDEAS.	ASSOCIATION.			TRANSFORMATION.	
	Mode.	Order.	Form.	Precedent word.	Subsequent word.
1	Imagining.	Proper.	Affirmative.	Representing.	Representing.
2	Denoting.	Proper.	Affirmative.	Representing.	Representing and composing.
3	Imagining	Exceptional.	Affirmative.	Representing.	Representing.
4	Denoting.	Proper.	Negative.	Representing.	Representing.
5	Attributing.	Proper.	Expressive.	Representing.	Representing.
6	Denoting.	Proper.	Affirmative.	Representing.	Representing.
7 ...	Denoting.	Exceptional.	Affirmative.	Representing.	Representing.

C. DISCONNECTED WORDS.

I. RELATION OF DISCONNECTED WORDS TO THE LINKING METHOD.

In the application of the registering method (Chapter I.) it was mentioned that to memorize disconnected words it is very necessary to apply a combined use of the linking and composing methods. Now the details and explanations in regard to the disconnected words are given, and no particular remarks will be made as to the composing methods. A disconnected word consists of two or more simple or connected words. Thus, to memorize a disconnected word we must associate them according to the fifth diagram (§ 1) by the operation of the linking or composing methods. Therefore, the disconnected words have a close relation with the linking and composing methods, and for this reason the following explanation will be given here.

II. CLASSES OF THE DISCONNECTED WORDS.

The disconnected word is one that consists of many simple or connected words having no relation or connection with each other. There are two classes of the present word, *i.e.*, the disconnected words of the first class and those of the second class.

a. The Disconnected Words of the First Class.

The words which belong to this class are those the meaning of which we can easily understand in spite of the fact that they include either simple or connected words; for instance:

1. The products of Japan: silk, coal, wood, and fish
2. Bamboo, beef, lake, and watch

There are one connected word and four simple words in the first example, and only four simple words in the second. The meanings of all the words contained in both examples are easy to be understood at one glance.

b. The Disconnected Words of the Second Class.

The words which belong to this class are those of which the meaning of each element included cannot be easily understood without special observation, for instance:

1. Ben P Cunningham
2. Hicksbeech Strandon
3. Sam Tam, Yam Yem, China

In these cases we cannot easily understand how many simple and connected words there are included in every disconnected word. However, they belong to a disconnected word as well as those in the first class They are very different from the first class in their characters, as they are quite unknown or unfamiliar words to us. On this account it is very necessary to adopt the two different methods for them.

III. EXAMPLES FOR MEMORIZING THE DISCON-
NECTED WORDS.

(A.) OF DISCONNECTED WORDS OF THE FIRST CLASS.

I Words to be Memorized.

1. Products of Japan silk, coal, wood, fish
2. Bamboo, beef, lake, watch
3. China, Russia, United States, Corea, Germany.

II. Linking

The associations between each simple or connected word included in a disconnected word of the first class are formed in the same manner as in associating ordinary simple or connected words, and the links of association are the same as shown in the fourth and fifth diagrams (§ 1). Thus, in the present examples, in order to associate the several words in the first group with those of the second, and the second with the third, that is, fish with bamboo, and watch with China, we shall associate them according to the first scheme given in the fifth diagram, or products of Japan with bamboo, and bamboo with China, according to the second scheme given in the fifth diagram. The practical exercise is left to the reader.

(B.) OF MEMORIZING DISCONNECTED WORDS OF THE SECOND CLASS.

I Words Required to be Memorized

1 Ben P Cunningham
2 Hicksbeech Strandon
3 Sam Tam, Yam Yem, Sang ing
4 He flies in the face of Providence

II. Transformation

a Special Rules for Transformation

The transformation of the disconnected words is accomplished by transforming a disconnected word which seems meaningless into some familiar simple or connected words, according to the mode given. There are very important points relating to the practice of the transformation of disconnected words. It is most convenient first to select the largest portion which can be easily transformed into a simple or connected word from the disconnected word required to be transformed. Secondly, a disconnected word can be transformed into several other words, and it is very important to transform the original words into some other words that have connections which can be easily associated with each other. For this reason the following points should always be observed:

1. When disconnected words are transformed, if there is a large portion which can be easily transformed into some simple or connected word, first select it, whether it is in the first or in the second or other parts, in a disconnected word, and then transform the rest.

2. Care must be taken to transform the original words into the new words which can be easily associated by having close relation between them.

b Practice of the Transformation

1 Given words .   Ben   P   Cunningham
   Transformed words . Bench Pea Cunning hammer

2 Given words . . . Hicksbeech Strandon
   Transformed words . Big Speech, Strand dam

3 Given words . . Sam Tam, Yam Yem, Sang ing
   Transformed words . Sun Tan, Young Aim, Singing

4 Given words . . . *He flies in the face of Providence*
   Transformed words . . Heat flying deface   officer Providence

LINKING METHOD. 69

c Explanation.

1. (a) "Ben" is transformed into "bench" and "P" into "pea" by the adding transformation.
   (b) "Cunningham" is divided into "cunning" and "ham"
2. (a) "Hicksbeech" is divided into "Hick" and "sbeech" and "Hick" is transformed into "big" and "sbeech" into "speech" by analogous sound.
   (b) "Strandon" is divided into "stran" and "don," "stran" is transformed into "strand" by adding transformation, and "don" into "dam" by transformation by analogous sound
3. (a) "Sam" is transformed into "sun" by transformation by analogous sound, "tam" into "tan" by transformation by analogous sound.
   (b) "Yam" is transformed into "young" and "Yem" into "aim" by the transformation by analogous sound
   (c) "Sang ing" is transformed into "singing" by changing and composing transformations
4. (a) "He" is transformed into "neat" by adding transformation "Fly" and "in" are transformed into "flying" by transformation by analogous sound.
   (b) "The" and "face" are transformed into "deface" by the transformation by analogous sound, and "of" into "officer" by the adding transformation
   (c) "Providence" is not transformed because we supposed it to be more convenient not to change it in regard to following associations.

III Linking

By means of transformation the disconnected words that seem to have no meaning were transformed into the words which can be easily understood. To associate them there is no difference between this case and the simple and connected words.

1. (a) *Bench* is covered by the *pea vine*
   (b) *Pea flowers* are variegated by *human cunning*
   (c) *Cunning fox* stole *ham*
2. (a) Big speech was made on the strand
   (b) The *broken strand* made a *dam* in the river

3. (a) *Sunshine* sometimes looks *tan color*.
   (b) *Tan color* is often liked by *young aimless one*.
   (c) *Young aimless men* are *singing* in the yard.
4. (a) By *heat flying* insects were killed.
   (b) *Flying* insects *defaced* an *officer*.
   (c) Then officer was rescued by *Providence*.

IV. ANALYSIS OF LINKED IDEAS.

NO. OF IDEAS.	ASSOCIATION.			TRANSFORMATION.	
	Mode.	Order.	Form.	Precedent word.	Subsequent word.
1. (a)	Imagining.	Proper.	Affirmative.	None.	Composing.
(b)	Denoting.	Proper.	Affirmative.	Composing.	Composing.
(c)	Imagining.	Proper.	Affirmative.	Composing.	None.
2. (a)	Imagining.	Proper.	Affirmative.	Composing.	None.
(b)	Imagining.	Proper.	Affirmative.	Composing.	None.
3. (a)	Denoting.	Proper.	Affirmative.	Composing.	Composing.
(b)	Imagining.	Proper.	Affirmative.	Composing.	Composing.
(c)	Imagining.	Proper.	Affirmative.	Composing.	None.
4. (a)	Imagining.	Proper.	Affirmative.	None.	None.
(b)	Imagining.	Proper.	Affirmative.	Composing.	None.
(c)	Imagining.	Proper.	Affirmative.	None.	None.

(C.) MEMORIZING DISCONNECTED WORDS OF THE FIRST AND SECOND CLASSES.

Memorizing disconnected words is comparatively the most difficult, therefore another example will be given in order that the readers may thoroughly understand the subject.

I. DISCONNECTED WORDS TO BE MEMORIZED.

1. Charles Hill, Main Street, London.
2. James White, Doctor of Medicine of Cambridge University.
3. Seneca Street, Ithaca City, Cayuga County, New York.
4. American cities, Washington, New York, Chicago, Philadelphia, Boston, and San Francisco.
5. English cities, London, Liverpool, Glasgow, Dublin.
6. Oriental countries, Japan, China, Corea, India.

LINKING METHOD.

II Transformation

1. Given words . . . . Charles Hill, Main Street, London.
   Transformed words   Charges, Bill, chain,   lantern.
2. Given words . . James White, Doctor of Medicine, Professor
   Transformed words . Fame, white, doctor of medicine, professor.
         of   Cambridge University
       well off, gamble, rich, university
3. Given words . . . . Seneca Street, Ithaca City, Cayuga, New York
   Transformed words   snake,   easy, car,   care, gun, New York.
4. Given words   American cities,   Washington, New York,
   Transformed words   United States,   Washington, new, work,
         Chicago, Philadelphia, Boston, San Francisco
         cargo, filled, ale, beer, button, sun, frank, risk
5. Given words . . . English cities, London, Liverpool, Glasgow,
   Transformed words   Inn, greasy,   lantern, river, poor, grass, goat,
         Dublin
       double ring.
6. Given words . . Oriental countries, Japan, China, Corea,
   Transformed words   East,   rising sun, shine, coral,
         India
         India

III Linking

1. (a) To demand *charge* a merchant sent me a *bill*
   (b) The *bill* was for a watch *chain* that I bought
   (c) The *chain* to carry the *lantern* was destroyed
2. (a) To get a *great fame* man must work till his hair becomes *white*.
   (b) A *white-haired doctor of medicine*
   (c) That *doctor of medicine* is a *professor of university*
   (d) *Professors* are *well off*
   (e) Man who is *well off* does not *gamble*
   (f) *Gambling* sometimes makes a man *rich*
   (g) A *rich man* makes a large donation to a *university*
3. (a) Some *snakes* can be killed *easily*
   (b) It is not an *easy thing* to travel long on *horse-cars*
   (c) Man in a *car* must take *good care* of it
   (d) *Care* must be taken of *guns*
   (e) The *gun* was manufactured in *New York*

4. (a) *United States* owes very much to *George Washington.*
   (b) In *Washington* there is much *news*
   (c) *News writing* is *hard work*
   (d) *Working man* is carrying *cargo*
   (e) *Cargo* was *filled* with precious things
   (f) I *filled* a bottle with *ale*
   (g) *Ale* and *beer* are nearly the same
   (h) *Beer dealer* has *precious button*
   (i) *Gold button* shines great deal in the *sun.*
   (j) *New York Sun* describes a *frank man*
   (k) *Frank man* often *risks* his life.
5. (a) Table cloth in an *inn* was *greasy*
   (b) It is *greasy work* to clean a *lantern*
   (c) A boat with a *lantern* is sailing in the *river*
   (d) *River excursions* are convenient for *the poor.*
   (e) *Poor men* often sleep on *grass*
   (f) Some *grass* is needed to feed *goat*
   (g) *Goat horns* are in the shape of a *double ring*
6. (a) *Eastern sky* became scarlet by *rising sun*
   (b) *Rising sun shines* beautifully.
   (c) There is no *shine* in the *coral*
   (d) *Coral* is mostly produced in the *Indian Ocean*

N B —If it is required to memorize all the six disconnected words in the order according to the fifth diagram explained in the beginning of this chapter, associate the last word of the first disconnected word, "lantern," with the first word of the second disconnected word, "fame," as "*lantern* is used in *famous party*," or associate the first word of the first disconnected word, "charge," with the first word of the second, "fame," as: "How do you *charge* for this *famous cutlery?*" The rest can be associated in the same way.

§ 3.—Linking and Registering Methods.

In memorizing disconnected words we always find it very convenient to apply both linking and registering methods, one of which cannot have any use without the other. Hence, when we desire to memorize many disconnected words we should link each single or connected word which is included in each disconnected word by the linking method, and these disconnected words should be associated by the registering method, and it is very convenient to use these two methods at the same time. Hence:

A. DIFFERENCE BETWEEN LINKING AND REGISTERING METHODS.

It has been already said that if we use both methods at the same time it is very convenient, but if they are used separately, the nature of each method and the effect is more or less changed. The difference will be explained as follows:

1. The linking method is originated from the first, third, fourth, and fifth rules (Chapter I , Part I.), while the registering method is originated from the first, second, and fifth rules. In other words, the linking method is the process of associating with each other the matters required to be memorized, while the registering method is to memorize the matters by associating them with the objects already existing in memory

2. In the linking method each matter is material to the formation of two associations, except the first and last ones, while in the registering method each matter can be only a material of one association

3. When many matters are required to be memorized by the linking method some of the associations sometimes will not be clear, while there is no such danger in the registering method

4 By the linking method numberless objects can be memorized in right order, while in the registering method the number of objects can be no more than the number of words in the register, and thus the matters for operation of the registering method cannot be numberless. But in the practical case there is no necessity to memorize numberless objects at once, and therefore this difference has no practical effect

5 In the memory obtained by the linking method it is difficult to recollect instantly the order or number of the objects, or to recite them in every direction, while it is very easily done by the registering method.

6 The linking method can be most conveniently used in associating with each other simple or connected words included in a disconnected word, while the registering method is most convenient to associate each disconnected word in its right order.

74 MNEMONICS.

B. COMBINED APPLICATION OF THE LINKING AND REGISTERING METHODS.

I. Disconnected Words to be Memorized and Diagram of the Application.

1. REGISTER AND DIS-
   CONNECTED WORDS .. *A* .. Charles Hill, Main Street, London City.
   Charges, bill, chain, lantern.

   DIAGRAM ....

2. REGISTER AND DIS-
   CONNECTED WORDS .. *B* .. James White, Doctor of Medicine, Professor of Cambridge University.
   Famous, White, doctor of medicine, professor, well off, gamble, rich, university.

   DIAGRAM ....

3. REGISTER AND DIS-
   CONNECTED WORDS .. *C* .. Seneca Street, Ithaca City, Cayuga County.
   Snake, easy, car, care, gun.

   DIAGRAM ....

4. REGISTER AND DIS-
   CONNECTED WORDS .. *D* .. American cities, Washington, New York, Chicago, Philadelphia, Boston, San Francisco.
   United States, Washington, news, work, cargo, filled, ale, beer, button, sun, frank, risk.

   DIAGRAM ....

N.B.—In the above diagrams the double lines denote the application of the registering method, and single lines that of the linking method.

LINKING METHOD.

(II.) **Association Formed by the Combined Application of the Registering and the Linking Methods.**

a. Registration Formed by the Registering Method.

1. (A—charges) An *able man* was *charged* with political crime
2. (B—fame) A *big fame*
3. (C—snake) *Ceiling* was covered with paper having the figure of a *snake*
4. (D—United States) *Deer* brought from the *United States*

b. Linking.

The association between the simple and connected words included in the above disconnected words has been given in the preceding example of the application of the linking method. (*Vide ut supra.*)

C. SIMPLE APPLICATION OF THE REGISTERING METHOD TO THE DISCONNECTED WORDS.

Disconnected words may also be memorized by the registering method alone. In this case the disconnected words of the second class must be transformed equally as in the case of the application of the linking method, and the simple or connected words thus transformed should be associated in right order into the words of the register equally as in the case of registering the original simple or connected words; but there are two important points to be observed in this case:

I. We must select at once the most adaptable register according to the nature, form, or size of the disconnected words, or we must construct a register adaptable to the words which require to be memorized.

II. We must arrange the disconnected words in right order into the words of the register. On the contrary, if we select a register which is not adapted to the nature, form, or size of the disconnected words or the distribution is not proper the following inconveniences will occur:

a. The associations formed are not clear and certain;

b. The sphere of each disconnected word becomes very indistinct;

c. The orders of the association cannot be proper.

We will have an example of the operation of the registering method regarding disconnected words as follows:

Example
I. DISCONNECTED WORDS REQUIRED TO BE MEMORIZED.

1 Charles Hill, Main Street, London.
2 James White, Doctor of Medicine, Professor of Cambridge University.
3 Seneca Street, Ithaca City, Cayuga County.
4 American cities: Washington, New York, Chicago, Philadelphia, Boston, San Francisco.

II. TRANSFORMATION

1 Given words . . . . Charles Hill, Main Street, London
  Transformed words . charges, bill, chain, lantern

2 Given words . . . . James White, Doctor of Medicine, Professor
  Transformed words   fames, white, doctor, of, medicine, professor,
                      of   Cambridge   University
                      office, gamble, rich, university

3 Given words . . . Seneca Street, Ithaca City, Cayuga County.
  Transformed words . snake, easy, car, care, gun

4 Given words . . . American cities: Washington, New York,
  Transformed words . United States, Washington. News, work,
  Chicago, Philadelphia, Boston, San Francisco.
  cargo, filled, ale, beer, bottom, san, frank, risk

III SELECTION OF REGISTER AND THE DISTRIBUTION OF DISCONNECTED WORDS.

In the transformation, it is found that in each of the first and third disconnected words five words are involved; in the second, nine; and

LINKING METHOD

in the fourth, thirteen Therefore we can best adapt a register consisting of some of the consonants with the five vowels for the first and third, and for the second disconnected word, consisting of ten words, we shall adopt two series of consonants, and for the fourth, consisting of less than fifteen words, we shall adopt three series of consonants.

IV REGISTER

1 Ba, be, bi, bo, bu
2 Ca, ce, ci, co, cu, da, de, di, do, du
3 Fa, fe, fi, fo, fu
4 Ga, ge, gi, go, gu, ha, he, hi, ho, hu, ja, je, ji, jo, ju

V REGISTRATION OF THE DISCONNECTED WORDS

a Registration of the First Disconnected Word

1 (Ba—charges)   *Banker s charges*
2 (Be—bill)   *A bird was eating beans by its bill*
3 (Bi—chain)   *Bill for gold chain*
4 (Bo—lantern)   *Boat with a lantern*

a Registration of Second Word

1. (Ca—fame)   *A captain's fame*
2 (Ce—white)   *Ceiling is white*
3 (Ci—doctor of medicine) *Cider is recommended by doctor of medicine*
4 (Co—professor)   *College professor*
5 (Cu—office)   *Nice cucumbers were brought to the office*
6 (Da—gamble)   *Dangerous gambling*
7 (De—rich)   *The dentist is rich*
8 (Di—university)   *Large diamonds are shown in the university*

c Registration of Third Word

1 (Fa—snake)   *A famous show of snakes*
2 (Fe—easy)   *To recover from fever is not easy*
3 (Fi—car)   *Fire burnt a car*
4 (Fo—gun)   *A fox was shot with a gun*

d. Registration of Fourth Word.

1. (Ga—United States)   *Games* are popular in the *United States.*
2. (Ge—Washington)   *George Washington.*
3. (Gi—news)   A *giant* was reading the *news.*
4. (Go—work)   To get *gold* one must *work.*
5. (Gu—cargo)   *Guns* were sent as *cargo.*
6. (Ha—filled)   The *hay wagon* is *filled.*
7. (He—ale)   *Health* is improved by *ale.*
8. (Hi—beer)   In the *hill* I drank *beer.*
9. (Ho—button)   *Hole* for *button.*
10. (Hu—sun)   I was *hurt* by the *sun.*
11. (Ja—frank)   *Japanese* are *frank.*
12. (Je—risk)   *Jealousy* sometimes brings a *risk.*

CHAPTER III.

COMPOSING METHOD.

§ 1.—Explanation of the Method.

THIS is for composing a series of simple, connected, and disconnected words, or those included in a disconnected word, into one main idea.

EXPLANATION.—The composing method is almost equal to the linking method, in that it requires that words be associated two by two and in right order, but as it composes a sentence there must be a certain meaning in the whole series. The following diagrams denote the application of this method:

1. Simple words . . . . ○—○—○—○—○

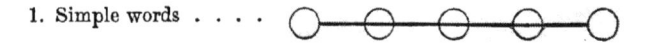

2. Connected words . . ◎—◎—◎—◎—◎

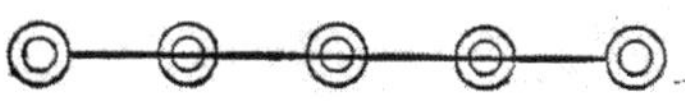

COMPOSING METHOD.

3. Simple and connected words . . . . . .

4. Disconnected words .

5. Simple, connected, and disconnected words . . . . .

The lines penetrating the rings in the above diagrams represent the main idea required for the composing method. Rings represent simple words, double rings connected words, and dotted lines disconnected words.

§ 2.—Application of the Method.

A. SIMPLE WORDS.

a. Words Required to be Memorized.

1. Vase.
2. Noise.
3. Maid-servant.
4. Garden.
5. Bat.
6. Wise.
7. Gold.
8. Flower.
9. Looking.
10. Mountain.

b. Composition.

"In a room where a *vase* is laid a great *noise* was heard, and then a *maid-servant* came to open the window. From the window I looked at the *garden*. There a *bat* was flying and a *wise*-looking girl, with *golden* hair and whose face was beautiful as a *flower*, caught it while she was *looking* at the *mountain*."

c. Explanation of the Composition.

1. Main idea or gist,—looking from a room.
2. The number of associations formed in the composing method is the same as in the case of the linking method. There ten simple words, as in

the above example, require nine associations, and in the above composition it is easily understood that there are nine associations. The modes applied for these formations of associations are only two; the five associations from the first to the fifth, and two associations, eighth and ninth, were formed by the imagining mode, and the two associations, sixth and seventh, attributing mode

B. CONNECTED WORDS.

a. Words Required to be Memorized.

1. Time is money.
2. The pen is mightier than the sword.
3. My bonnie lies over the sea.
4. Union forever.
5. Bacon and potatoes
6. Hear the sledges with their bells—silver bells.
7. General George Washington
8. Once upon a midnight dreary
9. A rolling stone gathers no moss

b. Composition

"Once upon a *time* I sent a small sum of *money*, *pen*, and *sword* to my bonnie, who lives along the *sea* washing the coast of the *United States* Then she brought *bacon* and *potatoes* to entertain me. We rode on a *sledge* with *silver bells* and went to a grave-yard where *George Washington* lies. This ride was very pleasant to us, and we drove until *midnight*, and took home with us some beautiful *moss*"

c. Explanation of Composition.

1. Main idea or gist,—the circumstance that one made a visit
2. The explanation of the transformation and association is left to the readers

C. DISCONNECTED WORDS

a. Words Required to be Memorized

1. George Hunter.
2. Charles Mason.
3. James Cobden.
4. Richard Roe
5. John Doe
6. Jane Wicoff.
7. William Thompson.
8. Lily Campbell
9. Jack Molton.
10. Annie Hutchins.

COMPOSING METHOD.

b. Transformation.

1.	Given words	George	Hunter,
	Transformed words	Geology	Hunter
2.	Given words	Charles	Mason,
	Transformed words	Charm	Mason.
3.	Given words	James	Cobden,
	Transformed words	Jam	Cob, den
4.	Given words	Richard	Roe,
	Transformed words	Rich, yard	Roe
5.	Given words	John	Doe,
	Transformed words	Join	Door
6.	Given words	Jane	Wicoff,
	Transformed words	Jean	Wicker, cough
7.	Given words	William	Thompson,
	Transformed words	Will	Ton, some
8.	Given words	Lily	Campbell,
	Transformed words	Lily	Camel
9.	Given words	Jack	Molton,
	Transformed words	Jacket	Melt, town
10.	Given words	Annie	Hutchins,
	Transformed words	Honey	Hat, chains.

c. Composition.

"For the investigation of *geology* I went to the mountains with a *hunter* who had a *charm* that showed that he was a *Mason*. We took bread and *jam* for lunch, but there were many *cobwebs* in a *den* that we went into, so we sat on the *rich* grass about fifty *yards* away and frightened a *roe* that was eating there. A man *joined* us who was standing in the *door* of a house close by; he had on *jeans* and had a *wicker* basket in his hand. He began to cough, and I said, "*Will* you help us to get a *ton* of some *lily* that I saw?" He took off a *camel's* hair *jacket* that he had on, as the snow was beginning to *melt* and it was warm. We then returned to the *town*, where I bought some *honey*. I took off my *hat* to them and picking up my *chains* went home."

d. Explanation

Main idea,—investigation of geology

§ 3.—Difference Between Linking and Composing Methods.

I. The linking method associates words to be memorized two by two, while the composing method associates words to be memorized into a main idea or a gist; in other words, the linking method forms an association of ideas between the first and second words, and between the second and third words, and so on. There is no relation between the associations made of the first and second words, and those made of the second and third words. In the composing method the association formed between the first and second words is closely related to the third word, or the association formed between the first, second, and third words is also related to the fourth word, and so on; the association formed between the first and second words and the association formed between the first association and the third word cannot be different from each other, as it is impossible to separate them. It is believed that the difference between them will become clearer by the following diagrams:

Diagram of Association of Ideas Formed by Linking Method

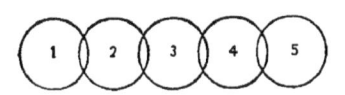

Diagram of Association of Ideas Formed by Composing Method.

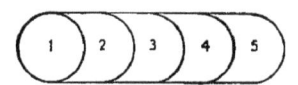

II. Associations formed by the linking method have an independent meaning between them individually, and associations formed by the composing method are pervaded by a main meaning, and they collectively form a series of sentences, as in the following diagrams:

Linking Method.

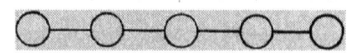

Each line represents an association individually independent in meaning.

Composing Method.

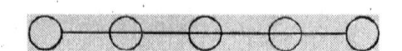

A long penetrating line represents a main idea weaving through all the associations.

III. The association by the linking method is formed quicker than that by the composing method in practice.

IV. The association formed by the composing method is firmer than that formed by the linking method and is able to preserve it longer.

V. When the subject is required to be memorized in an instant, and it is not necessary to preserve the memory for a long time, the linking method will be properly applied. When the memory of the subject is required to be preserved for a long time and it is not required to be memorized in an instant, the composing method will be conveniently applied.

§ 4.—Difference between Composing and Registering Methods.

I. Each word memorized by the registering method becomes a material of one association, while each word memorized by the composing method becomes material for one or more associations. Thus, in one composition which included ten associations formed according to the order by the composing method, the first and second words are used ten times as the materials for forming associations, and the third word nine times, fourth word eight times, and so on. The diagram of associations used for explaining the difference between the linking and the composing methods is also applied to explain this case.

II. The first, fourth, and fifth differences existing between the linking and the registering methods equally exist in the present case.

§ 5.—Combined Application of the Methods.

A. OF COMPOSING AND LINKING METHODS.

I. Diagrams of the Combined Application.

1. For Simple and Connected Words.

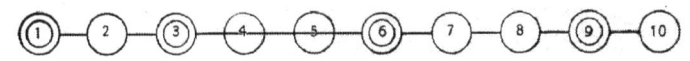

①—2—③—4—5—⑥—7—8—⑨—10

2. For Connected and Disconnected Words.

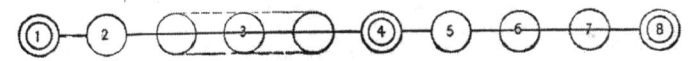

①—2—③—④—5—⑥—7—⑧

II. Examples of Combined Association.

a. Examples Corresponding to the First Diagram.

1. Words Required to be Memorized.
   1. Bring back my bonnie to me.
   2. City.
   3. Oliver Cromwell.
   4. Sword.
   5. Whale.
   6. Twinkle, twinkle, little star.
   7. Pen.
   8. Cyclone.
   9. War of Independence.
   10. Mnemonics.

COMPOSING METHOD.

2 Linking and Composition.

1. My *bonnie* is in some *city*
2. The *city* was the place where *Oliver Cromwell* was born
3. *Oliver Cromwell's sword* once cut a large *whale* under *star*-light. (Composing method.)
4. The *star* shines like a gold *pen*
5. A *pen* was blown off by a *cyclone*
6. *Cyclone* was like *War of Independence*
7. *War of Independence* is *memorized* by every one

b. Examples Corresponding to the Second Diagram.

1 Words Required to be Memorized

1. They tell us, sir, that we are weak
2. Train
3. Main Street, San Francisco
4. Hear the sledge with the bells—silver bells
5. Newspaper
6. Waterfall
7. Tobacco
8. There are many rare abilities in the world that fortune never brings to light

2 Transformation

Original word	Main Street,	San Francisco
New word	chain,	sun, frank, risk.

N. B.—One disconnected word only required transformation.

3 Linking and Composition.

1. A *weak man* was in the *train*
2. When a *large train* joined by *chain* ran towards the *sunset*. A *frank man* thought it a *risk*   (Composing method.)
3. A *risk* was experienced by a man on a *sledge*
4. A man on a *sledge* forwarded *newspapers*
5. A *newspaper* describing a *large waterfall* in some place was read by a man for *tobacco* who was a man of *ability*.   (Composing method.)

86   MNEMONICS.

B. COMBINED APPLICATION OF REGISTERING, LINKING, AND COMPOSING METHODS.

I. Diagrams of the Combined Application and its Examples.

1. REGISTER AND DIS-
   CONNECTED WORDS.. *A* .. Charles Hill, Main Street, London City.
                             Charges, bill, chain,   lantern.

   DIAGRAM . . . . . .

2. REGISTER AND DIS-
   CONNECTED WORDS. *Rolling* . James White, Doctor of Medicine, Professor of Cambridge University.
                                Famous, White, doctor of medicine, professor, well off, gamble, rich, university.

   DIAGRAM . . . . . .

3. REGISTER AND DIS-
   CONNECTED WORDS. *Stone* . Seneca Street, Ithaca City, Cayuga County, New York.
                              Snake,   easy, car,   care, gun,   news, work.

   DIAGRAM . . . . . .

COMPOSING METHOD. 87

I. **Diagrams of the Combined Application and its Examples.**
(Continued.)

4. REGISTER AND DIS-
   CONNECTED WORDS. *Gathers*. American cities, Washington, New York, Chicago, Philadelphia, Boston, San Francisco.
   United States, Washington, news, work, cargo, filled, ale, beer, bottom, sun; frank, risk.

   DIAGRAM . . . . . .

5. REGISTER AND DIS-
   CONNECTED WORDS. . *No* . . . English cities, London, Liverpool, Glasgow, Dublin.
   Inn, greasy, lantern, river, poor, grass, goat, double ring.

   DIAGRAM . . . . . .

6. REGISTER AND DIS-
   CONNECTED WORDS. *Moss* . Oriental States, Japan, China, Corea, India.
   East, rising sun, shine, coral, India.

   DIAGRAM . . . . . .

N.B.—In the above diagrams parallel lines represent the application of the registering method, short lines represent that of the linking method, and the penetrating lines represent that of the composing method.

II. Registration, Linking, and Composition.

1. (a) My *axe* was *charged* at five dollars (Registering method)
   (b) I looked at the *charges* that were demanded by a *bill* under the light of a *chained lantern* (Composing method)
2. (a) Invention of *rolling* machine gave great *fame* (Registering method)
   (b) A *white*-haired *doctor of medicine*. (Linking method)
   (c) *Doctor of medicine* was *professor of university* (Linking method.)
   (d) *Well-off* men do not *gamble* (Linking method)
   (e) *Gambling* sometimes makes men *rich* (Linking method)
   (f) A *rich* man made a large donation to a *university* (Linking method.)
3. (a) I *stoned* a *snake*. (Registration.)
   (b) I shot a *snake* easily from a *car*, taking good *care* of a *gun* bought in *New York* (Composing)
4. (a) I *gathered* postage-stamps of the *United States* (Registration)
   (b) *United States* owes very much to *George Washington*. (Linking)
   (c) In *Washington* there is much news (Linking)
   (d) *News*-writing is hard *work* (Linking)
   (e) *Workman* is carrying *cargo*. (Linking)
   (f) *Cargo* was *filled* with something (Linking.)
   (g) I *filled* a bottle with *ale* (Linking)
   (h) *Ale* and *beer* are similar (Linking)
   (i) Keeper of a *beer-stand* who is noted for his big diamond *button* got on the train after *sunset* As he was too *frank*, he thought it is a *risk* (Composing)
5. (a) A *noisy inn* (Registration)
   (b) The table-cloth in an *inn* was *greasy* (Linking)
   (c) It is *greasy work* to clean a *lantern* (Linking)
   (d) A boat with a *lantern* was sailing in a *river* (Linking)
   (e) A *river excursion* is very convenient for *poor men* (Linking)
   (f) A *poor* man often sleeps on *grass* (Linking)
   (g) Some *grass* is used to feed the *goat* (Linking)
   (h) The horns of a *goat* are the shape of *double rings* (Linking)
6. (a) I found much *moss* on the *east side* of the river. (Registration)
   (b) *Eastern sky* became clear by the light of the *rising sun* (Linking)
   (c) *Rising sun shines* very beautifully (Linking)

(d) There is not much *shine* in *coral*   (Linking)
(e) The *coral* is found in the *Indian Ocean*. (Linking)

N B —In the practical application, sometimes we require the combined application of three methods, and sometimes that of two, and sometimes the simple application of either one of them We cannot exactly describe the relation between the matters to be memorized and the methods to be properly applied to them Therefore it is very important to select practically the most convenient method to be applied to the matters by looking over the nature, form, and size of them

PART III.

APPLICATION OF THE METHODS IN REGARD TO SPECIAL OBJECTS.

CHAPTER I.

MEMORIZING NUMERALS.

§ 1.—Transformation.

ALL the numerals have not the necessary meaning to be applied with several methods, as has been stated in the preceding part. Therefore for memorizing numerals, unless the transformation is first applied to convert them into some other words, they cannot properly be taken as the material for association. At one glance it seems to be impossible to transform such numerals as 5, 8, 9, 15, 37, 67, 398, and 781, etc., into such words as have proper meaning, but every one can succeed very easily, quickly, and practically by the application of the transformation, observing some special points which will be explained in the present section.

A. TRANSFORMATION OF DIGITS.

This is the process of representing each digit by a letter and simple word.

The representing letters must be consonants. The representing letters and simple words and their origin will be explained in the following table:

TABLE I.

Number.	Representing letter.	Origin.	Transformation.	Representing simple word.	Transformation.
"0"	"r."	zero.	Selected letter.	"roe."	Adding.
"1"	"b."	beginning.	Different word and selected letter.	"bee."	Adding.
"2"	"t."	two.	Selected letter.	"tea."	Adding.
"3"	"d."	"drei." (German.)	Different word and selected letter.	"day."	Adding.
"4"	"f."	four.	Selected letter.	"foe."	Adding.
"5"	"c."	"cinq." (French.)	Different word and selected letter.	"cake."	Adding.
"6"	"s."	six.	Selected letter.	"sea."	Adding.
"7"	"p."	"septem." (Latin.)	Different word and selected letter.	"ape."	Adding.
"8"	"g."	eight.	Selected letter.	"age."	Adding.
"9"	"n."	nine.	Selected letter.	"knee."	Adding.

Explanation of Table.

1. "0" is represented by "r" because "r" is taken from the third letter of "zero" by transformation by selected letters. The representing simple word of "o" may be "roe," "air," etc., made by adding transformation.

2. "1" is represented by "b," which is the first letter of "beginning," which resembles "one" in some respects. This change is made by transformation by different word and by selected letter. The representing simple word may be "bee," formed, as before, by adding transformation.

3. "2" is represented by "t," from "two," and the representing word may be "tea," etc., etc.

N.B.—In the present transformation consonants only are taken as representing characters, and the vowels are used commonly as the auxiliary for composing some simple words by these representing characters.

The representing simple word is made by adding vowels to the representing consonant, while the consonants "j," "k," "q," "x," "y," and "z" are used the same as the vowels, for they are not in this system taken to represent anything

B. TRANSFORMATION OF NUMERALS IN TWO ORDER.

The numerals in two order means all the numbers between 10 and 99. These numbers should be transformed into simple words, and for this purpose the representing letter of each digit, as above explained, is taken as the principal element. In associating the representing letters of the digits when the representing simple words of numerals in the two order are made, the vowels should always be used freely as auxiliary letters between both representing characters or before or after them. On the contrary, the auxiliary consonants are entirely prohibited, except j, k, q, x, y, and z, but there is no objection to using them after both representing characters for composing simple words, because the first two consonants of every simple word composed are only representing characters of the numerals, and the other consonants have no relation to them. Several examples for composing the representing simple words are given, as follows: To connect "t" and "d" the vowel "i" is inserted between the characters and "e" is added after "d." By this process the noun "tide" is made, representing the numeral "23." Sometimes two vowels are inserted between the representing characters; for instance, "b" and "f" are connected by composing the noun "beef," representing the numeral "14." Sometimes both representing characters are connected without the intervention of vowels, but have vowels following them, as "s" and "t" are composed into the word "stone," representing "62." Sometimes a vowel is put before the repre-

MEMORIZING NUMERALS.

senting characters; for instance, to connect "f" and "f" a word affinity is composed representing "44." When we recollect that two representing characters are composed for some words, by either of these methods the first two consonants only are taken into consideration. Supposing the word "dictionary" is composed; it includes d, c, t, n, and r, all being representing characters of numerals, but "d" and "c" in the first part only are taken into our consideration, representing "35." The consonants v, l, h, m, and w are used for other purposes which will be explained in another place. The consonants j, k, q, x, y, and z are not used for the purpose of representation in consequence of their inability to compose a word, but may be used as auxiliaries.

The most important point, which should always be held in mind, is that all the simple words representing the numerals in two order must be nouns. If we compose an adjective, verb, or any other kind of word by the representing letters it causes a great confusion in our memory.

REPRESENTING LETTERS AND WORDS OF THE NUMERALS IN TWO ORDER.

N.B.—There cannot be some independent numerals, as "00," "01," etc, but in the practice of memorizing numerals we may always have such independent numerals, which are the result of the long series of numerals divided. Therefore in this system these numerals are treated the same as the other numerals in two order, as in the following table

TABLE II.

Original numbers	0	01	02	03	04	05	06	07	08	09
Representing characters	r.	r, b.	r, t.	r, d.	r, f.	r, c.	r, s.	r, p.	r, g.	r, n.
Simple words	rear, arrow, or error.	ribbon, rabbit, or robber.	root, rat, or earth.	radish, ridicule, or order.	roof, rifle, or refreshment.	race, rice, or rock.	rose, restaurant, or rascal.	rope, repair, or orphan.	rag, rage, or organ.	rain, ring, or rent.
Original numbers	10	11	12	13	14	15	16	17	18	19
Representing characters	b, r.	b, b.	b, t.	b, d.	b, f.	b, c.	b, s.	b, p.	b, g.	b, n.
Simple words	bear, beer, or brush.	bible, baby, or abbey.	bat, boat, or boot.	bed, body, or abdomen.	beef, buffalo, or buffoonery.	back, bacon, or beach.	basket, bus, or bosom.	baptism, Baptist.	bag, beggar, or bug.	bone, banner, or bank.
Original numbers	20	21	22	23	24	25	26	27	28	29
Representing characters	t, r.	t, b.	t, t.	t, d.	t, f.	t, c.	t, s.	t, p.	t, g.	t, n.
Simple words	torch, tear, or trade.	table, tobacco, or tub.	tooth, tutor, or attorney.	tide, tadpole, or toad.	tiffin, tuft, or taffy.	teacher, tackle, or technics.	taste, Tuesday, or toast.	top, tapioca, or tippler.	tiger, tug, or tagrag.	tin, tongue, or tennis.
Original numbers	30	31	32	33	34	35	36	37	38	39
Representing characters	d, r.	d, b.	d, t.	d, d.	d, f.	d, c.	d, s.	d, p.	d, g.	d, n.
Simple words	drunkard, deer, or direction.	debt, doubt, or debauchery.	duty, date, or ditch.	dodge, dead, or address.	deaf-mute, defeat, or difficulty.	duck, doctor, or dictionary.	desert, desk, or disease.	diploma, diplomat, or depot.	dog, dagger, or digestion.	dinner, danger, or dentist.
Original numbers	40	41	42	43	44	45	46	47	48	49
Representing characters	f, r.	f, b.	f, t.	f, d.	f, f.	f, c.	f, s.	f, p.	f, g.	f, n.
Simple words	fruit, forest, or foreigner.	February, fable, or fabric.	foot, fatigue, or father.	food, fidelity, or fodder.	effect, affection, or affliction.	face, fact, or fiction.	fist, fish, or feast.	fop.	fog, fig, or figure.	fan, finger, or fence.

MEMORIZING NUMERALS.

Original numbers	50	51	52	53	54	55	56	57	58	59
Representing characters	c, r.	c, b.	c, t.	c, d.	c, f.	c, c.	c, s.	c, p.	c, g.	c, n.
Simple words	car, corn, or curtain.	cabin, cable, or cob.	cat, cottage, or actor.	cod, academy, or cider.	cuffs, coffee, or coffin.	cock, account, or accident.	coast, cash, or cost.	cap, copper, or captain.	cigar, cigarette, or cognac.	coin, cane, or candle.

Original numbers	60	61	62	63	64	65	66	67	68	69
Representing characters	s, r.	s, b.	s, t.	s, d.	s, f.	s, c.	s, s.	s, p.	s, g.	s, n.
Simple words	sardine, sorrow, or source.	subject, sabbath, or sob.	street, storm, or stone.	soda, seed, or saddle.	safe, suffering, or suffocation.	scissors, science, or scenery.	sister, ass, or suspender.	soap, soup, or spring.	sugar, sigh, or sign.	son, snake, or song.

Original numbers	70	71	72	73	74	75	76	77	78	79
Representing characters	p, r.	p, b.	p, t.	p, d.	p, f.	p, c.	p, s.	p, p.	p, g.	p, n.
Simple words	park, pork, or price.	public, puberty, or publication.	pot, patent, or path.	pudding, pedler, or paddock.	puff, pfenning.	pocket, picture, or package.	pistol, post, or paste.	paper, pipe, or pepper.	pig, pagan, or pugilist.	pin, pen, or pony.

Original numbers	80	81	82	83	84	85	86	87	88	89
Representing characters	g, r.	g, b.	g, t.	g, d.	g, f.	g, c.	g, s.	g, p.	g, g.	g, n.
Simple words	girl, garden, or ground.	gobbler, goblet, or Gibbon.	gate, goat, or gatling-gun.	god, goods, or guide.	gift, gaff, or guffaw.	go-cart, gaucherie, or guaiacum.	gas, goose, or guest.	gape, gypsy, or gap.	egg, gig, or geography.	gun, ginger, or gentleman.

Original numbers	90	91	92	93	94	95	96	97	98	99
Representing characters	n, r.	n, b.	n, t.	n, d.	n, f.	n, c.	n, s.	n, p.	n, g.	n, n.
Simple words	north, nurse, or nourishment.	noble, nubia, or nobility.	net, nut, or nature.	end, needle, or undertaking.	information, enforcement, or infidelity.	neck, uncle, or nickname.	nose, nest, or insect.	nephew, nippers, or napkin.	night, negro, or engagement.	noon, nonsense, or nun.

The simple words in the preceding table are furnished for examples only. The reader may compose any other simple words out of the representing characters according to the process of transformation which he may consider most suitable to the case. And this is more easily done if he is a little trained in the application of transformation. Thus the reader is required to make his own table of simple words representing the numerals from "00 to 99," and in the above table it is not necessary to memorize all the words, but it perhaps includes the most common and principal ones, which should be adopted as the representative characters in the present case.

N.B.—Some may consider that it is impossible to memorize a table composed like that on pages 94 and 95. This is a great mistake, however. The simple words in the table are those which may instantly be composed upon a glance at the representing characters. There is no such difficulty as you may imagine when required to memorize every representing character, because they are very closely related to the original.

C TRANSFORMATION OF THE NUMERALS IN THREE ORDER.

The numerals in three order include the whole series of numerals between "000" and "999." They have all three representing characters, therefore all of them cannot be transformed into simple words, for there is one more representing character to be composed, besides two representing characters which can be transformed into a simple word, as already explained in the preceding paragraph. Then it is necessary to transform this one remaining character into a simple word and to associate it with the other simple word composed of two representing characters. To compose them this one remaining character should be transformed into an adjective, the simple word composed of the two representing characters being necessarily a noun, as explained in the preceding paragraph, and an adjective is associated very easily with a noun. For this reason the numerals from "0" to "9" should at first be transformed into adjectives, and they will be associated with the simple words representing the numerals from "00" to "99," as the case may require.

1 Transformation to Adjectives

1. The representing character "r" may be transformed by adding transformation into red, right or rare, rotten, etc

2. The representing character "b" may be transformed by adding transformation into beautiful, bad or blue, bashful, etc.

3. The representing character "t" may be transformed by adding transformation into tall, thin or terrible, thick, timid, troublesome, etc.

4. The representing character "d" may be transformed by adding transformation into dark, dirty or deep, dry, etc.

5. The representing character "f" may be transformed by adding transformation into fine, fair, funny, etc.

6. The representing character "c" may be transformed by adding transformation into clean, cheap or careless, etc.

7. The representing character "s" may be transformed by adding transformation into small, short, stale, slow, etc.

8. The representing character "p" may be transformed by adding transformation into pure, poor, pleasant, etc.

9. The representing character "g" may be transformed by adding transformation into good, great, greasy, gay, etc.

10. The representing character "n" may be transformed by adding transformation into new, noble, narrow, near, etc.

TABLE III.

Original number; its division	0/00	0/01	0/02	0/03	0/04	0/05	0/06	0/07	0/08	0/09
Representatives	r, r r.	r, r b.	r, r t.	r, r d.	r, r f.	r, r c.	r, r s.	r, r p.	r, r g.	r, r n.
Connected word	rare arrow.	red ribbon.	rare rat.	right order.	rare rifle.	rare rock.	red rose.	rare rope.	rare organ.	rare ring.
Original number; its division	0/10	0/11	0/12	0/13	0/14	0/15	0/16	0/17	0/18	0/19
Representatives	r, b r.	r, b b.	r, b t.	r, b d.	r, b f.	r, b c.	r, b s.	r, b p.	r, b g.	r, b n.
Connected word	red bear.	rare abbey.	red boat.	red body.	rare buffalo.	red back.	red basket.	rare Baptist.	red bag.	red banner.
Original number; its division	1/00	1/01	1/02	1/03	1/04	1/05	1/06	1/07	1/08	1/09
Representatives	b, r r.	b, r b.	b, r t.	b, r d.	b, r f.	b, r c.	b, r s.	b, r p.	b, r g.	b, r n.
Connected word	beautiful arrow.	beautiful ribbon.	bad rat.	bad order.	beautiful rifle.	bad rice.	beautiful rose.	bad rope.	beautiful organ.	beautiful ring.
Original number; its division	1/10	1/11	1/12	1/13	1/14	1/15	1/16	1/17	1/18	1/19
Representatives	b, b r.	b, b b.	b, b t.	b, b d.	b, b f.	b, b c.	b, b s.	b, b p.	b, b g.	b, b n.
Connected word	bad brush.	bad baby.	beautiful boat.	beautiful bed.	bad beef.	bad bacon.	beautiful basket.	bad Baptist.	beautiful bag.	blue banner.
Original number; its division	2/00	2/01	2/02	2/03	2/04	2/05	2/06	2/07	2/08	2/09
Representatives	t, r r.	t, r b.	t, r t.	t, r d.	t, r f.	t, r c.	t, r s.	t, r p.	t, r g.	t, r n.
Connected word	terrible error.	thin ribbon.	terrible rat.	terrible order.	tall roof.	tall rock.	tall rascal.	thin orphan.	thin rag.	terrible rain.

98 MNEMONICS.

MEMORIZING NUMERALS

Original number, its division	2/60	2/61	2/62	2/63	2/64	2/65	2/66	2/67	2/68	2/69
Representatives	t, s r	t, s b	t, s t.	t, s d	t, s f	t, s c	t, s s	t, s p.	t, s g	t, s n
Connected word	terrible sorrow.	tall subject	terrible storm	thin saddle	tall safe	terrible scenery	thin sisters.	thin soap	tall sign	tall son

Original number, its division	3/20	3/21	3/22	3/23	3/24	3/25	3/26	3/27	3/28	3/29
Representatives	d, t r	d, t b.	d, t t	d, t d	d, t f	d, t c	d, t s	d, t p	d, t g	d t n
Connected word	dirty trade	dirty table	dirty tooth	dirty toad	dirty tuft.	dirty tackle	dirty toast.	dirty tippler.	dirty tug	dirty tin

Original number; its division	3/30	3/31	3/32	3/33	3/34	3/35	3/36	3/37	3/38	3/39
Representatives	d, d r	d, d b.	d, d t.	d, d d	d, d f	d, d c.	d, d s	d, d p	d, d g	d, d n
Connected word	dirty deer	dark doubt	deep ditch	dirty deads	dirty deaf-mute	dirty duck.	dark desert	dark depot	dirty dog	dirty dentist

Original number, its division	4/40	4/41	4/42	4/43	4/44	4/45	4/46	4/47	4/48	4/49
Representatives	f, f r	f, f b	f, f t	f, f d.	f, f f	f, f c	f, f s	f, f p	f, f g	f, f n
Connected word	fair foreigner.	fine fabric.	fine foot	fine food	fine effect	funny face	fine fish	funny fop	fine fig	fine fan

Original number; its division	4/50	4/51	4/52	4/53	4/54	4/55	4/56	4/57	4/58	4/59
Representatives	f, c r	f, c b	f, c t.	f, c d	f, c f	f, c c	f, c s	f, c p.	f, c g	f, c n
Connected word	fine car	fine cable.	fine cat	fine cider	fine cuffs	fine cock	fair coat	funny cap	fine cigar	fine cane

TABLE III.—Continued.

Original number; its division	Representatives	Connected word
5 60	c, s r.	clean sardine.
5 61	c, s b.	careless subject.
5 62	c, s t.	clean street.
5 63	c, s d.	cheap saddle.
5 64	c, s f.	clean safe.
5 65	c, s c.	cheap scissors.
5 66	c, s s.	cheap suspenders.
5 67	c, s p.	clean soap.
5 68	c, s g.	clean sugar.
5 69	c, s n.	careless son.

Original number; its division	Representatives	Connected word
5 70	c, p r.	clean park.
5 71	c, p b.	careless publics.
5 72	c, p t.	clean pot.
5 73	c, p d.	clean pudding.
5 74	c, p f.	careless puff.
5 75	c, p c.	clean package.
5 76	c, p s.	cheap pistol.
5 77	c, p p.	clean paper.
5 78	c, p g.	careless pugilist.
5 79	c, p n.	cheap pen.

Original number; its division	Representatives	Connected word
6 80	s, g r.	small garden.
6 81	s, g b.	small goblet.
6 82	s, g t	small gate.
6 83	s, g d.	small goods.
6 84	s, g f.	small gift.
6 85	s, g c.	small go-cart.
6 86	s, g s.	small goose.
6 87	s, g p.	short gypsy.
6 88	s, g g.	small egg.
6 89	s, g n.	small gun.

Original number; its division	Representatives	Connected word
6 90	s, n r.	small nurse.
6 91	s, n b.	short noble.
6 92	s, n t.	small nut.
6 93	s, n d.	small undertaking
6 94	s, n f.	stale information.
6 95	s, n c.	short uncle.
6 96	s, n s.	small insect.
6 97	s, n p.	small napkin.
6 98	s, n g.	short negro.
6 99	s, n n.	small nun.

Original number; its division	Representatives	Connected word
7 00	p, r r.	poor arrow.
7 01	p, r b.	poor rabbit.
7 02	p, r t.	poor rat.
7 03	p, r d.	pure order.
7 04	p, r f.	poor rifle.
7 05	p, r c.	pure rice.
7 06	p, r s.	poor rascal.
7 07	p, r p.	poor orphan.
7 08	p, r g.	poor organ.
7 09	p, r n.	poor ring.

MEMORIZING NUMERALS.

Original number, its division	7 10	7 11	7 12	7 13	7 14	7 15	7 16	7 17	7 18	7 19
Representatives	p, b r	p, b b	p, b t	p, b d	p, b f	p, b c	p, b s	p, b p	p, b g	p, b n
Connected word	pure beer	poor baby	poor boat	poor bed	pleasant buffoonery	pleasant beach	poor basket	pure Baptist	poor beggar	poor bank
Original number, its division	8 20	8 21	8 22	8 23	8 24	8 25	8 26	8 27	8 28	8 29
Representatives	g, t r	g, t b	g, t t	g, t d	g, t f	g, t c	g, t s	g, t p	g, t g	g, t n
Connected word	great trade	good tobacco	good tooth	great toad	good tiffin	good teacher	good taste	good tapioca	great tiger	good tin
Original number; its division	8 30	8 31	8 32	8 33	8 34	8 35	8 36	8 37	8 38	8 39
Representatives	g, d r	g, d b	g, d t	g, d d	g, d f	g, d c	g, d s	g, d p	g, d g	g, d n
Connected word	great deer	great debt	great duty	good address	great difficulty	good doctor	great desert	great depot	good dog	good dinner
Original number, its division	9 40	9 41	9 42	9 43	9 44	9 45	9 46	9 47	9 48	9 49
Representatives	n, f r	n, f b	n, f t	n, f d	n, f f	n, f c	n, f s	n, f p	n, f g	n, f n
Connected word	new fruit	new fabric	noble father	new food	new effect	noble face	new fish	noble fop	new fig	new fan
Original number, its division	9 60	9 61	9 62	9 63	9 64	9 65	9 66	9 67	9 68	9 69
Representatives	n, s r	n, s b	n, s t	n, s d	n, s f	n, s c	n, s s	n, s p	n, s g	n, s n
Connected word	new sardine	new subject	new street	new saddle	new sate	new scissors	new suspenders	new soap	new sign	new song

2. Transformation to Connected Word

The first character out of three may usually be transformed into an adjective and the following two characters into a simple word; for instance, in the numeral "123" the first character, "1," may be transformed into "beautiful," as in the above explanation, and the following "23" may be transformed into "tadpole," as in the second table. Thus a connected word, "beautiful tadpole," is composed by combining, then representing the number "123," and so on. Examples of connected words made in this way are given in Table III.

N B —1 The reader can easily make out of the representing letters any adjective which will be considered most suitable for the composition of connected words, but care must be taken not to make two or more adjectives which have equal or analogous meaning For instance, "beautiful" out of "b" and "nice" out of "n" are the same in many cases, which may be very confusing when memorizing.

2 Table III describes a portion of the whole series between 000 and 999 and provides examples The reader may try to complete the table by his own labor There cannot, of course, be such independent numbers as 000 or 001, but they are always found in the transformation of such numbers as 23,000 or 56,001, they being divided into simple and connected words by the lines drawn under them

D. TRANSFORMATION OF THE NUMERALS CONSISTING OF THE SAME NUMERAL CHARACTERS IN MORE THAN TWO ORDER.

Any numerals may have a series consisting of tne same numerical letters, for instance, 111, 222, 333, 4444, 55555, 88888888, etc. In these cases a special method is required, *i.e.*, a connected word representing many of the same numerals. For this purpose a simple word is first made between a character denoting number of the same numerals in a series and a character representing each numeral itself in a series, as in the second table. Secondly, at the head of the simple word made in this way an adjective, "many," is added, then a connected word is composed; for instance: "111" is three "1's," and the representing characters for them are "d" and "b," which are to be associated into a simple word, "debt." The adjective "many" being added before it, they compose a connected word, "many debts." Six "5's" are represented by the two characters, "s" and "c," or a simple word, "sack," and when the word "many" is added to it a connected word, "many sacks," is composed. Unless the adjective "many" be added to the simple word an error will instantly occur, that is, "d" and "b" in the first example may be mistaken for 31 instead of three "1's," *i.e.*, "111." But the adjective "many" avoids this difficulty, because this adjective is specially used for this case.

TABLE IV.

Original numbers	111	222	3333	44444	555555	6666666	77777777
Representatives	many d b.	many d t.	many f d.	many c f.	many s c.	many p s.	many g p.
Connected word	many debts.	many duties.	many foods.	many cuffs.	many socks.	many pistols.	many gypsies.

When the series of the same numeral characters of more than eight order is required to be memorized the same rule applies. For instance: fifteen "5's," namely, are "15, 5," that are represented by "b, c c." In this case "c c" may be associated to form a simple word and "b" may be made an adjective, so as to form a connected word. The adjective "many" may again be put before the connected word. Thus "c c" compose a word, "cock," and "b" an adjective, "beautiful." A connected word formed by them is "beautiful cock," and the adjective "many" is added to it, and "many beautiful cocks" represents a series consisting of fifteen "5's." In another example eighteen "7's" are represented by "b, g p." They were first composed into a connected word, "big gypsies," and again into "many big gypsies," another connected word which has two adjectives.

For the present case another different method will be applied; that is, three "1's" are represented by "dead bee," and four "2's" by "fine tea," and so on.

E TRANSFORMATION OF THE NUMERALS CONSISTING OF ZEROS IN MORE THAN TWO ORDER.

In the numerals in more than three order there may be numbers containing zeros in more than two order. In such cases the above method is applied. For instance, three zeros may be transformed into "d" and "r," "d" representing three and "r" representing zeros. These two representing characters are associated to a word, "deer," and a connected word, "many deer," represents "000," and so on.

TABLE V.

Original numbers	000	0000	00000	000000	0000000	00000000	000000000
Representatives	d r	f r	c r	s r	p r	g r	n r
Connected word	many deer	many fires	many cars	many surgeons	many pears	many girls	many nurses

F. TRANSFORMATION OF THE NUMERALS IN THE FOUR OR MORE ORDER.

As already explained, the numerals in one and two order may all be transformed into simple words, and the numerals themselves may be called simple words. All numerals in three order may be transformed into connected words, and the numerals themselves may be called connected words.

The numerals in more than three order cannot be transformed into simple or connected words, but they are changed into disconnected words, for they all include many simple or connected words. For instance: the numerals in four order include two simple words which have no relation to each other; those in five order include one simple and one connected word; those in six order include three simple words or two connected words, those in seven order include two simple words and one connected word; those in eight order include four simple words or two connected words and one simple word. They must be transformed into such simple or connected words as are equal to the disconnected words, as already explained, and to memorize the transformed parts they must be associated with each other by the linking or composing methods. In the following pages the numerals in more than three order are called the numerals in many orders.

I. TRANSFORMATION.

1. Special Rules Concerning Transformation of Numerals in Many Orders.

1. Divide the numerals into simple words as much as possible.

2. After the memorizer is accustomed to the application of the transformation he can use either simple or connected words by dividing numerals according to his desire.

2. Examples

a TRANSFORMATION FOR NUMERALS IN FOUR AND FIVE ORDERS.

1	Original numerals ..	59	42
	Disconnected words ..	cane	fatigue
2	Original numerals ..	38	76
	Disconnected words ..	dog	pistol

MNEMONICS.

3	Original numerals ...	46	35	
	Disconnected words ..	fish	doctor	
4	Original numerals ..	90	05	
	Disconnected words	nourishment	rice	
5	Original numerals ...	10	90	
	Disconnected words ..	beer	nourishment	
6	Original numerals ...	50	009	
	Disconnected words ..	car	rare ring	
7.	Original numerals ..	39	348	
	Disconnected words ..	dinner	dirty fig	
8	Original numerals ..	98	000	
	Disconnected words ..	negro	many deer	
9	Original numerals ...	67	777	
	Disconnected words ..	soaps	many depots	
10	Original numerals ..	530	59	
	Disconnected words ..	careless deer	cane	

b. For Numerals in Six to Ten Orders.

1	Original numerals ..	580	057		
	Disconnected words ..	careless girls	rare cap		
2.	Original numerals ...	300	52	59	
	Disconnected words ..	dark rear	cottage	candle	
3	Original numerals ..	90	000	520	
	Disconnected words ..	nurse	many deer	cheap torch	
4	Original numerals ...	35	666666		
	Disconnected words ..	doctor	many sisters		
5	Original numerals .	39	000000		
	Disconnected words ..	dentist	many surgeon		
6.	Original numerals ..	464	825	78	
	Disconnected words ..	fine safe	good teacher	pig	
7	Original numerals ...	998	853	970	
	Disconnected words ..	noble negro	good cider	new park	
8	Original numerals	300	09	000	99
	Disconnected words ..	dark rear	ring	many deer	noon
9	Original numerals ..	9999	000000		
	Disconnected words ..	many fan	many surgeon		
10	Original numerals ...	209	003	05	07
	Disconnected words	terrible rain	red radish	rock	orphan

II. EXERCISE FOR MEMORIZING.

This exercise should have been given under § 3 in the order of the explanation, but for convenience and to make it more easily understood it was inserted here.

Associations in the present examples are the same as those of the simple and connected words included in a disconnected word. They are formed by the linking and composing methods.

a. Associations of the Preceding Examples Transformed.

1. The *cane* diminishes *fatigue*
2. A *dog* was shot with a *pistol*
3. The *fish* which a *doctor* likes to eat
4. There is *nourishment* in *rice*
5. *Beer* is *nourishing*
6. A man on a *car* had a *rare ring*
7. The *dinner* has a *dirty fig*
8. A *negro* hunts *many deer*
9. The *soap* was advertised in *many depots*
10. A careless *deer* was beaten with a *cane*

b. Associations Formed of the Example for the Numerals from Six to Ten Grades

1. A careless girl with a rare cap
2. The *dark rear* of a *cottage* must be lighted by *candle*
3. A *nurse* looks at *many deer* under the light of a *cheap torch*
4. A *doctor* has *many sisters*
5. A *dentist* has *many surgeons* as friends
6. I saw in a store of *fine safes* a good teacher attending *pigs*
7. A *noble negro* was drinking *good cider* in the *new park*
8. In the *dark rear* they gave *rings* to *many deer* at noon.
9. *Many fans* were given to the sick by *many surgeons*.
10. In a *terrible rain* I went out to buy a *red radish*, and near a *rock* I saw an *orphan*

§ 2.—Transformation of Numerical Words Denoting the Numeration.

If the numerals required to be memorized have no decimals or fractions there seems to be no necessity of numerating, for we can easily tell how many orders they have by counting the representing characters. For example: one character is in the order of units; two characters denote the order of tens; three characters are in order of hundreds; four characters denote the order of thousands, and so on. Even in such a case, however, a long series of characters needs a routine, instead of numbering the characters one after the other in order to know their order. If you err in the numbering, the order is instantly mistaken. Therefore numerating is necessary, even in the numerals above the units. But when the numerals have decimals or fractions, to memorize them is practically useless, unless they are rightly numerated. Suppose there is a numeral, "8990," which may be formed into a composed idea, "Ginger is brought by nurse." This association may easily recall the numeral, but it will be very difficult to memorize the orders of it, as when they may have such different orders,—8,990 or 899.0 or 89.90 or 8.990 or .8990. Thus, unless you know that the way in which the order of the numeral is memorized is the same as in memorizing the numerals themselves your memory has no value. The author, knowing this difficulty, suggests the following method of numeration:

A. TRANSFORMATION OF NUMERATION INTO LETTERS

1. Million is represented by "w."
2. Thousand is represented by "m."
3. Hundred is represented by "h."
4. Unit is represented by "l."
5. Fraction is represented by "v."

B. ORIGIN OF THE REPRESENTING CHARACTER.

1. "W" is the first letter of the word wealth, representing the word million. The word million is first transformed into millionaire by adding transformation and again transformed into wealth by transformation by different words. This is taken for the representation of million.

2. "M" is the Latin letter denoting a thousand, and this is taken for the representation of the word thousand by transformation by different word.

3. "H" is the first character of the word hundred, and is selected as its representative.

4. "L" is the first character of the word lowest. Unit is the lowest order of numerals above decimals; therefore the word unit is transformed into the word lowest order by transformation by different word, in which "l" is selected to represent the whole.

5. "V" is the third character of the word divisor. The word fraction is transformed into the word divisor by transformation by different words which are closely related to the denominator of the fraction, and the character "v" is selected to represent the whole.

C TRANSFORMATION OF THE REPRESENTING CHARACTERS OF NUMERATION INTO ADJECTIVES

These representing characters may be associated with every representing character of the numeral to compose a simple word. For instance, the representing characters of one million are "b" and "w," and they compose a word, "bow." For fifty million two hundred thousand there may be "c, r, w, t," composing two words, "car" and "water." The representing letter of numeration may often be before two representing characters of the numeral to be associated with them, composing a connected word. In this case it must form an adjective. For instance, seventeen hundred twenty-one may be "b, p, h, t, b," and for transforming them into a simple and connected word, "h" is first transformed into an adjective, "heavy;" then they compose the words "Baptist" and "heavy table." The adjectives made of the representing characters of the order are as follows:

TABLE VI.

Original word	million.	thousand.	hundred.	unit.	fraction.
Representatives	w.	m.	h.	l.	v.
Transformed word	worthy, wonderful.	mad, merry.	heavy, hard.	large, long.	violent, various.

In the case of decimals the representative of the unit will be in the foremost position, and next will come that of the decimal. For instance, 25.33 will be "t, c, l, d, d" and .582 "l, c, g, t."

In the case of fractions the representative of the unit will be in the foremost position, next will come the representative of the numerator, next the representative of the fraction, and in the last the representative of the denominator. For instance, 25¾ will be "t, c, l, d, v, f." These orders must not be altered.

D. SIMPLE WORDS WHICH CONSIST OF COMBINING THE REPRESENTATIVES OF THE NUMERATIONS AND THOSE OF THE NUMERALS.

The following table gives an example of the simple words. The reader may make another table for himself which he may consider more conveniently according to the above explanation.

MEMORIZING NUMERALS.

TABLE VII.

		zero and fraction.	1 and fraction.	2 and fraction.	3 and fraction.	4 and fraction.	5 and fraction.	6 and fraction.	7 and fraction.	8 and fraction.	9 and fraction.
FRACTION	Original words										
	Representatives	r, l.	b, v.	t, v.	d, v.	f, v.	c, v.	s, v.	p, v.	g, v.	n, v.
	Simple words	river, raven, or ravage.	bivouac or beverage.	tavern.	diver, divorce, or dove.	fever or favor.	cover, cavalry, or cave.	savage, sovereign, or souvenir.	poverty, pavement, or pivot.	government, governor, or gavel.	novel, novelist, or novice.
	Original words	fraction and zero.	fraction and 1.	fraction and 2.	fraction and 3.	fraction and 4.	fraction and 5.	fraction and 6.	fraction and 7.	fraction and 8.	fraction and 9.
	Representatives	v, r.	v, b.	v, t.	v, d.	v, f.	v, s.	v, s.	v, p.	v, g.	v, n.
	Simple words	varlet or vermifuge.	vibration.	veteran or veterinarian.	vaudeville, vedette, or evidence.	vifsa, or vifrous.	victim or vaccination.	vest or vase.	vapor.	vegetable or vagabond.	avenue, oven, or venison.
UNIT	Original words	zero and unit.	1 and unit.	2 and unit.	3 and unit.	4 and unit.	5 and unit.	6 and unit.	7 and unit.	8 and unit.	9 and unit.
	Representatives	r, l.	b, l.	t, l.	d, l.	f, l.	c, l.	s, l.	p, l.	g, l.	n, l.
	Simple words	rail, religion, or relative.	balloon, billiard, or bell.	tool, telegram, or tall.	deluge, dealer, or doll.	flower, fool, or flour.	ceiling, clam, or cellar.	silk, soldier, or slope.	police, plant, or play.	gold, glove, or gallery.	nail or inlet.
	Original words	unit and zero.	unit and 1.	unit and 2.	unit and 3.	unit and 4.	unit and 5.	unit and 6.	unit and 7.	unit and 8.	unit and 9.
	Representatives	l, r.	l, b.	l, t.	l, d.	l, f.	l, c.	l, s.	l, p.	l, g.	l, n.
	Simple words	larceny, lyre, or lard.	library, laborer, or lobster.	letter, leather, or lot.	ladder, lady, or lad.	leaf or life-boat.	alcohol, lace, or lacquer-ware.	lass, list, or ulster.	leper, leopard, or lip.	leg, light, or log.	lion, linen, or lung.
HUNDRED	Original words	zero and hundred.	1 and hundred.	2 and hundred.	3 and hundred.	4 and hundred.	5 and hundred.	6 and hundred.	7 and hundred.	8 and hundred.	9 and hundred.
	Representatives	r, h.	b, h.	t, h.	d, h.	f, h.	c, h.	s, h.	p, h.	g, h.	n, h.
	Simple words	rheumatism, rhetoric, or rehearsal.	behavior, bohea, or abhorrence.	throat, thunder, or thirst.	adhesion or dahlia.	Fahrenheit.	child, church, or chalk.	shoulder, shrimps, or sheep.	photograph, pharmacist, or pheasant.	ghost or gherkin.	Nihilist, inhabitant, or inherence.

MNEMONICS.

TABLE VII.—Continued.

		hundred and zero.	hundred and 1.	hundred and 2.	hundred and 3.	hundred and 4.	hundred and 5.	hundred and 6.	hundred and 7.	hundred and 8.	hundred and 9.
HUNDRED	Original words	h, r.	h, b.	h, t.	h, d.	h, f.	h, c.	h, s.	h, p.	h, g.	h, n.
	Representatives	horse, horn, or herring.	habit, bubble, or hubbub.	hat, heat, or hatchet.	bread, hedge, or hodge-podge.	heifer, hoof, or haft.	hackberry, hack, or hiccough.	husband, hose, or hash.	happiness, hop, or hoop.	hog, hag, or height.	honey, hand, or honor.
	Simple words										
THOUSAND	Original words	zero and thousand.	1 and thousand.	2 and thousand.	3 and thousand.	4 and thousand.	5 and thousand.	6 and thousand.	7 and thousand.	8 and thousand.	9 and thousand.
	Representatives	r, m.	b, m.	t, m.	d, m.	f, m.	c, m.	s, m.	p, m.	g, m.	n, m.
	Simple words	room, romance, or ram.	bamboo, bomb, or bumpkin.	time, tomb, or timber.	dome, domino, or dummy.	family, female, or famine.	camel, comet, or comb.	summer, seminary, or summit.	pump, pimple, or paymaster.	game, gambler, or gimlet.	name, number, or nominee.
	Original words	thousand and zero.	thousand and 1.	thousand and 2.	thousand and 3.	thousand and 4.	thousand and 5.	thousand and 6.	thousand and 7.	thousand and 8.	thousand and 9.
	Representatives	m, r.	m, b.	m, t.	m, d.	m, f.	m, c.	m, s.	m, p.	m, g.	m, n.
	Simple words	mirror, market, or merchant.	mob, mob-cap, or ambition.	mat, mother, or match.	medicine, mud, or madman.	muff or muffin.	machine, mechanics, or muck.	mast, museum, mist.	map, maple, or import.	magazine, magnet, or emigration.	man, mind, or monkey.
MILLION	Original words	zero and million.	1 and million.	2 and million.	3 and million.	4 and million.	5 and million.	6 and million.	7 and million.	8 and million.	9 and million.
	Representatives	r, w.	b, w.	t, w.	d, w.	f, w.	c, w.	s, w.	p, w.	g, w.	n, w.
	Simple words	reward, rowing, or rowen.	bow, bowel, or bowl.	towel, twin, or tweezers.	dew, dawn, or dower.	fowl or fawn.	cow, coward, or cowslip.	saw, sewing, or swallow.	pawn, powder, or power.	gown, gewgaw, or gawky.	news, newspaper, or newt.
	Original words	million and zero.	million and 1.	million and 2.	million and 3.	million and 4.	million and 5.	million and 6.	million and 7.	million and 8.	million and 9.
	Representatives	w, r.	w, b.	w, t.	w, d.	w, f.	w, c.	w, s.	w, p.	w, g.	w, n.
	Simple words	wit, work, or ware.	web or webbing.	water, watch, or weather.	wedding, widow, or weed.	wife, or wafer.	wicket or wick.	washing, west, or wisdom.	weapon or wiper.	wagon or wig.	wind, window, or wine.

MEMORIZING NUMERALS

E. TRANSFORMATION OF NUMERALS, DENOTING THE ORDERS.

I NUMERALS ABOVE TEN THOUSAND.

1 Example

1	687,950,000.
2	2,000,920,000
3	39,582,500,000
4	525,380,000,000
5	230,090,000,000
6	58,735.
7	590,370
8	5,000,035
9	90,030,703
10	15,520,937.

2 Transformation

1 Original number . 687, million 950, thousand
   Transformed words . short gypsy wonderful nickname
2 Original number . . 2,00   0, million 9   20, thousand
   Transformed words . terrible roar red window tear
3. Original number . 39,   58   2, million 5 00, thousand
   Transformed words . dinner cigar tall wicket
4 Original number . . . 525,   38   0, million.
   Transformed words careless teacher dog rowing
5. Original number . . 230,   09   0, million
   Transformed words tall drunkard ring rowing
6 Original number . 58, thousand   7 3 5
   Transformed words careless gambler   poor doctor
7 Original number . . . 590,   thousand 3   70
   Transformed words . careless nurse medicine park
8 Original number . . 5, million 000,0   35
   Transformed words cow many farmer doctor.
9 Original number 90, million 030,   703
   Transformed words nice row right direction pink radish.
10 Original number 15, million 520,   937
   Transformed words . bashful coward clean trunk new depot.

8

N B —For memorizing numeration of numerals the memorizers should not transform more than one word denoting numeration in each series of them, because it is enough to memorize the numeration for a series of numerals if either one of the representatives of numeration is memorized with those of the numerals

3 Exercise for Memorizing

(This exercise is inserted here for the reason given in the exercise for memorizing numerals of many orders)

1 A *short gypsy* having a *wonderful nickname*

2 A man making a *terrible roar* by a *red window* had a *tear* in his eye

3 After *dinner* I smoke a *cigar* near a *tall wicket*

4 A *careless teacher* with his dog went rowing

5 A tall drunkard wearing rings was rowing

6. The *careless gambler* was formerly a *poor doctor*

7 A *careless nurse* who went to buy *medicine* was in the *park*.

8. *Cows* owned by *many farmers* were treated by a *doctor*

9 A *nice row* in the *right direction* while eating a *pink radish*.

10. A *bashful coward* received a *clean trunk* in *new depot*.

4 Recollection of Numeration

When we want to recollect the order of the numerals we reckon the number of representing characters from right to left; starting at the representative character of numeration, the first character will denote units, the second tens, etc., in relation only to the representative character of numeration. For example, we have the idea—"A man making a terrible roar by a red window had a tear in his eye." We extract the representative characters and find t, r, r, r, w, n, t, r, or 2, 0, 0, 0, million, 9, 2, 0.

To recollect the order we start at the representative character of numeration, which is "w" in this case, and count to the left, units, tens, hundreds, thousands, which gives us two thousand million.

II. NUMERALS IN FOUR ORDER OR LESS AND THOSE WITH FRACTIONS OR DECIMALS.

1. Example

1	9,735 90
2	1,696 12
3	639 87
4	58.32,5
5	3 78,9
6	0 69,75
7	0 09,92
8	0 00,38,2
9	$350\frac{87}{120}$
10	$9\frac{3}{8}$

2 Transformation

1. Original number . . 9, thousand 7   35 9
   Transformed words . new import   dirty cane

2. Original number . 1, thousand 6   96.   12
   Transformed words . beautiful museum   nest   bat

3. Original number . . 6 hundred 3   9   87
   Transformed words . small head   noble gypsy

4. Original number . . 58 unit   325
   Transformed words   cheap glove   dirty teacher

5. Original number . 3. unit   7 8, 9
   Transformed words . dealer   pure ginger-ale.

6. Original number   unit 6 9,   7 5
   Transformed words   large snake package

7. Original number . . unit 0 9,   9 2
   Transformed words   large ring   nuts

8. Original number . . unit 0 0,   3 8, 2
   Transformed words . long arrow   dirty gate

9. Original number . 3   50   unit 3 7   fraction 1   20
   Transformed words   dirty car   large depot   vibration trip

10. Original number . . 9. unit   5 fraction 8
    Transformed words . inlet   clean vegetable

3. Exercise for Memorizing

(This is inserted here for the reason given in the preceding exercise.)

1. Among *new imports* there was a *dirty cane*
2. I saw in a *beautiful museum* a *nest of bats*.
3. I met a man of *small head* who was a *noble gypsy*.
4. A *cheap glove* worn by the *dirty teacher*
5. The *dealer* has a *pure ginger-ale*
6. A *large snake* in *package*
7. One who wears a *large ring* eats *nuts*
8. A *long arrow* found in a *dirty gate*
9. Because a *dirty car* to a *large depot* had vibration I gave up the trip.
10. In the *inlet clean vegetables* are found.

4. Recollection of Numeration.

In this case the numeration above from unit will be reckoned as already explained. To recollect the order of decimals, the representing character must be reckoned behind the unit; when a fraction has an integral number, to recollect the order of the numerator it should be reckoned behind the unit, and the denominator behind the representative of the fraction. Thus, if there be two representatives behind the unit and before the representative of the fraction, the numerator is in ten order; if there be two behind the fraction, the denominator also is in ten order.

§ 3.—Exercise in Memorizing Numerals.

Concerning the transformations of several preceding cases the following conclusions will be given for the readers' convenience:

I. The numerals in one and two orders are all transformed into simple words.

II. The numerals in three orders are transformed into connected words.

III. The numerals in more than three orders are transformed into a disconnected word.

IV. Every representing character of every numeral is transformed into simple and connected words, combining with each representing letter of numeration.

V. In the transformation of the numerals numerated the representing letter of the order takes a position as a numeral, and then the number of the characters representing numerals always increases by one. Therefore numerals of three order have four representing characters and those of four order have five, and so on. Thus, they being transformed into simple or connected or disconnected words, the exercise in the present case follows the same routine as that of the preceding part.

A MEMORIZING NUMERALS BY THE REGISTERING METHOD

1 EXAMPLES.

(1) 3 5 9.	(6) 9 8	(11) 3 9	(16) 7 6 6
(2) 4 0 5.	(7) 5 6	(12) 4 6 8.	(17) 9 6 7.
(3) 9 0 0	(8) 9 2 5	(13) 8	(18) 3 8 3.
(4) 2 8	(9) 3 9 9	(14) 1 9	(19) 7 7 7
(5) 2 2 2	(10) 9	(15) 5 9 8	(20) 5 1

N B.—Transformation of these numerals into simple or connected words already given is referred to the association

2 REGISTER.

ba, be, bi, bo, bu, ca, ce, ci, co, cu, da, de, di, do, du, fa, fe, fi, fo, fu.

3 REGISTRATION

1	(Baby—dirty cane)	A *baby* plays with a *dirty cane*
2	(Beggar—fine rock)	A *beggar* sitting on a *fine rock*
3	(Bill—new arrow)	A *bill* for a *new arrow*
4	(Bone—thin leg)	Bone of a *thin leg*
5	(Bull—many dots)	Bull has *many dots* on his skin.
6	(Cat—negro)	A *cat* owned by a *negro*
7.	(Ceiling—clean ulster)	The *ceiling* covered with *clean ulster's* cloth.
8	(Cider—new teacher)	*Cider* is liked by my *new teacher*
9	(Comb—dirty nun)	A *comb* owned by *dirty nun*
10	(Cucumber—knee)	A *cucumber* is on my *knee*
11.	(Date—dirty linen.)	The *date* wrapped in *dirty linen.*

12	(Deer—fine sugar)	The *deer* was eating *fine sugar*.
13	(Diver—age)	A *diver's age*
14	(Dog—bank)	A *dog* on the *bank*
15	(Dummy—clear night)	I met a *dummy* in a *clear night*.
16	(Face—poor sisters)	*Faces* of the *poor sisters*
17	(Fence—new soap)	*Fence* where *new soap* was found
18	(Fighting—dirty guides)	I saw the *fighting* of the *dirty guides*
19	(Fox—many dippers)	A *fox* was shot by a man carrying *many dippers*
20	(Fur—careless laborer)	*Fur* owned by a *careless laborer*.

4 EXPLANATION OF THE REGISTRATION

The explanation of the transformation of numerals and the associations applied are left to the reader's self study.

B MEMORIZING NUMERALS BY LINKING METHOD.

1 EXAMPLES.

The preceding examples are borrowed for the present purpose

2 LINKING.

1. A *dirty cane* was left near a *fine rock*
2. A *fine rock* was shot by a *new arrow*.
3. The *new arrows* carried by a man with *thin legs*
4. A man of *thin leg* with *many dots* on his clothes
5. *Many dots* were made by a *negro*
6. A *negro* wearing an *ulster*
7. *Ulster* worn by my *new teacher*
8. My *new teacher* loves a *dirty nun*
9. A *dirty nun* injured on the *knee*
10. The *knee* was covered by a *dirty linen*.
11. *Dirty linen* wrapping *fine sugar*
12. *Fine sugar* ordered by a *man of age*
13. The *man of age* was a *banker*.
14. A *banker* was walking on a *clear night*
15. A *clear night* when the *poor sisters* were singing
16. The *poor sisters* bought *new soap*
17. *New soaps* left by a *dirty guide*
18. The *dirty guide* has *many dippers*
19. The *many dippers* made by a careless laborer.

N B —The explanations of association applied in the above cases are all left to the reader.

C MEMORIZING THE NUMERALS BY COMBINED APPLICATION OF REGISTERING, LINKING, AND COMPOSING METHODS

1. EXAMPLES

1	49,825 90,01
2	99,990 00,12
3	3 92,5
4	775,300 00,1
5	. 5,389,376
6	. 500,000 99,1
7	0 35,75
8	100 $\frac{2\,3}{5\,0}$
9	3 90,92
10	0 00,03,5

2 TRANSFORMATION

1 Original number   49, thousand   8 2 5   9 0, 0 1
   Transformed words   . fine name   good teacher   , nurse ribbon.

2 Original number . . . four 9's   0 unit 0   0, 1 2
   Transformed words . many fans   rich lord   red boat

3 Original number   3 unit 9   2 5
   Transformed words   dreadful lion   teacher

4. Original number . . 7 7 5,   m 3 0   0 0   0, 1
   Transformed words   poor package mad drunkard   rarity   robber

5 Original number .   5, w 3   8 9, 3   7 6.
   Transformed words . cool woods   good Indian   pistol.

6 Original number . . . 5 0 0,   three 0's   unit 9   9, 1
   Transformed words   cruel arrow many deer   linen   noble,

7. Original number . . unit 3 5,   7 5
   Transformed words   large duck   package

8 Original number . 1 0 0   unit 2 3   fraction 5 0
   Transformed words   beautiful arrow   large toad   valuable cerate.

9 Original number   3. unit 9   0, 9 2
   Transformed words   dry linen   rich nuts

10 Original number   unit 0 0,   0 3, 5.
   Transformed words   large arrow   red duck.

3. Associations of Transformed Words by Linking and Composing Methods

1. One who has a *fine name* as a *teacher* rewarded a *nurse* with *ribbon*
2. *Many fans* purchased by a *rich lord* were carried away on a *red boat*
3. A *dreadful lion* bit a *teacher*
4. The *poor package* carried by a *mad drunkard* contained a *rarity* which was stolen by a *robber*.
5. In a *cool woods* a *good Indian* was shot with a *pistol*
6. *Cruel arrow* shot *many deer*. The *many deer* were attended by a boy wearing *linen* clothes. The *linen* was given by a *nobleman*
7. A *large duck* in a *package*
8. By a *beautiful arrow* one killed a *large toad*. The *toad* turned out to be *cerate*
9. *Dry linen* wrapping *rich nuts*
10. A *large arrow* hit a *red duck*

4. Registration of all Series by Registering Method.

a. Register

a, b, c, d, e, f, g, h, i, j.

b. Registration

1. (Ale—fine name)   *Ale* is made by men of *fine name*
2. (Bee—many fans)   *Bee* flying around the *many fans*
3. (Ceiling—dirty linen) The *ceiling* is covered by *dirty linen*.
4. (Doctor—poor package) A *doctor* brought a *poor package*
5. (East—cool woods)   *East* is surrounded by *cool woods*
6. (Fool—cruel arrows)   *Fool* is not afraid of *cruel arrows*
7. (Gate—large duck)   In *gate* I caught a *large duck*
8. (Hat—beautiful arrow) *Hat* was shot by *beautiful arrow*.
9. (Ice—dry linen)   *Ice* packed in a *dry linen*
10. (Joker—large arrow)   A *joker* carrying a *large arrow*

N B.—When it is required to memorize such numerals as the preceding example from dictation one must first prepare the register; secondly, associate the first word of first series with the register, thirdly, associate the words included in the first series with each other, and next go to the second series and so on.

MEMORIZING NUMERALS.   121

5. **Simple Application of Registering Method without Aid of Other Methods to the Present Examples.**

a. Selecting the Register.

It is clear enough at a glance that each series includes simple or connected words not more than five in number, and there are ten series. The register for this case requires the words of ten series, each series consisting of five words. The following register will satisfy the points required:

b Register

1 ba, be, bi, bo, bu   6 ha, he, hi, ho, hu
2 ca, ce, ci, co, cu   7 ja, je, ji, jo, ju
3 da, de, di, do, du   8 ka, ke, ki, ko, ku
4 fa, fe, fi, fo, fu   9. la, le, li, lo, lu
5 ga, ge, gi, go, gu   10 ma, me, mi, mo, mu.

c Registration

FIRST SERIES

1 (Baby—fine name)   *Baby* has a *fine name*
2 (Bee—good teacher)   *Bee* stings the *good teacher*
3 (Bible—nurse)   *Bible* owned by a *nurse*
4 (Bone—ribbon)   *Bone* fastened with a *ribbon.*

SECOND SERIES.

1 (Cat—many fan)   *Cat* playing with *many fans*
2 (Cellar—rich lard)   *Cellar* keeps *rich lard*
3 (Cider—red boat)   *Cider* is brought in the *red boat*

THIRD SERIES.

1 (Date—dirty linen)   *Dates* wrapped in a *dirty linen*
2 (Deer—teacher)   *Deer* is watched by *teacher*

FOURTH SERIES.

1 (Fan—poor package)   *Fan* is wrapped in a *poor package*
2 (Fence—mad drunkard)   *Fence* damaged by a *mad drunkard.*
3 (Fire—rarity)   *Fire* burned a *rarity*
4. (Fox—robber)   *Fox* killed by a *robber.*

FIFTH SERIES

1. (Gate—cool woods)   A *gate* is in the *cool woods*
2. (Gentleman—good undertaking)   *Gentleman* starts a *good undertaking*
3. (Giant—pistol)   *Giants* had a *pistol*.

SIXTH SERIES

1. (Hare—cruel arrows)   *Hare* is shot with *cruel arrows*.
2. (Head—many deer)   *Heads* of *many deer*.
3. (Hill—linen)   On the *hill* I saw heavy *linen*
4. (Horse—noble)   A *horse* owned by a *noble*

SEVENTH SERIES

1. (Janitor—large duck)   *Janitor* bought a *large duck*.
2. (Jewel—package)   *Jewels* found in a *package*.

EIGHTH SERIES

1. (Kangaroo—beautiful arrow)   A *kangaroo* was killed by a *beautiful arrow*.
2. (Kettle—large toad)   *Kettle* is put on *large toad*
3. (Kitten—valuable cerate)   A *kitten* carried out a *valuable cerate*.

NINTH SERIES.

1. (Lamb—dry linen)   *Lamb* covered with a *dry linen*.
2. (Lieutenant—rich nuts)   *Lieutenant* ate *rich nuts*

TENTH SERIES.

1. (Map—large arrow)   *Maps* were broken by a *large arrow*
2. (Menagerie—red duck)   In *menagerie* I saw a *red duck*.

CHAPTER II.

MEMORIZING FOREIGN LANGUAGES.

§ 1.—Special Rules for Transformation.

THE several rules for transformation of disconnected words are, of course, applicable to the foreign languages. But there are also some special rules which, together with the general rules, will be stated as follows :

RULE I.—Unfamiliar foreign words must be transformed into simple, connected, or disconnected familiar words, the transformation by identical or analogous sounds being mostly applied.

RULE II —In the transformation of foreign words with many syllables or letters, if you can find one or more familiar words consisting of many syllables or letters, first separate them from each other by dividing transformation, and transform the rest in the order of their prominence and length.

RULE III.—In the transformed words it is generally well to have as close a relation to the meaning of the original foreign words as possible.

RULE IV.—In the course of transformation if one whole familiar word cannot be found which is similar in sound to the whole or part of the given foreign word, the sound of only the first syllable of some familiar word or a connected sound consisting of the first syllables of two or more familiar words will be applied to the given foreign words to imitate the sound.

Under these rules there are some different cases, as follows :

MNEMONICS.

Examples

1 Japanese word "keng," which means "sword," is transformed into "cane," which is a whole English word similar in sound to the original word

2 Japanese word "mong," which means "gate" in English, is transformed into the sound "mong," which is first syllable of the word "monger" The sound "mong" to represent the word "monger" was selected, applying the transformation by selected letter.

3 Japanese word "yujin," which means "friend" in English, is transformed into a disconnected word "ewe" and "gin," in which the connected sound coincides with that of the original word, the transformation by identical sound being applied

4 The Japanese word "seiteng," which means "fine weather" in English, is transformed into the sound "sa-ten," formed by a connection with the first syllables of two words, "sable and tenant " The sound "sa-ten" represents the two words, "sable and tenant," by the representing transformation

RULE V.—If, however, some foreign words cannot be transformed into familiar words by the application of the preceding rules, the sound consisting of one or more of the beginning or the ending letters of an English word or a connected sound of those of two or more English words will be applied to imitate the sound of the given foreign word.

N B —In application of the above rule, the sound of the letter in the beginning of a word is preferred to that of the ending

Examples

1 The German word "Gedicht," which means "poem" in English, is transformed into a connected sound, "ga-di-hit," consisting of the first two letters of the words "gay" and "dignity" and of the word "hit."

2. The Russian word "nētsuka," which means "thread" in English, is transformed into a connected sound, "nee-ts-ka," consisting of the first three letters of the word "needle," and of the last two of the word "fruits," and of the first two of the word "cart "

RULE VI.—If the transformed words can be understood by each memorizer, it will be enough, however abnormal the changes may be.

Origin of the Preceding Special Rules

The preceding rules for memorizing unfamiliar foreign languages are based upon the similarity of the sound elements of the several languages. However much the languages may differ from each other, the single original sounds composing them are almost the same throughout the world. If we analyze any language on earth into single individual sounds, we will find that there are at most about one hundred original sounds which can be uttered by the organ of the human being, though there is some difference, either great or small, in these sounds when uttered by the same vocal organs in the different portions of the world. Therefore, although there are a great many different languages used in the world, it is very evident that they are composed by different arrangement and combination of the same single original sounds, with a few exceptions, some original sounds of one language not being used in another. What are these single original sounds? There are two different kinds of sound,—that of the consonants, which are uttered by each vocal organ without the aid of the other vocal organs, and that of the vowels, which are uttered naturally by a human being without a special act of the vocal organs. These simple original sounds can never again be divided, however earnestly we may try. For instance, the word "act" may be divided for the simple original sounds, "a-c-ts," which are uttered by different vocal organs, that is, "a" is uttered naturally without a special act of the vocal organs, "c" by the aid of the throat, and "ts" by the tongue with the palate. The word "hunt" may be divided for the simple sounds "h-u-n-t," which are uttered by the vocal organs, the throat, the nose, and the tongue, with the palate

But these simple original sounds cannot again be divided

into smaller sounds by our knowledge, and as these are generally used everywhere throughout the world, it will be understood that the several languages are similar to each other in regard to their original sounds. The sound "acts" in the preceding example coincides with the Japanese words "ac" and "tsu," which mean "bad" and "shore," and the sound "hunt" coincides with the Japanese word "hant," which means "territory" in English.

Examining as to how many simple original sounds there are in English,—that is to say, how many different kinds of vocal utterances are used in the pronunciation of the simple original sounds of the language,—we easily find that there are not more than about forty. The simple original sounds in English include twenty-one consonants and some other combined consonants, as "th," "ch," "sh," "wh," "ng," etc., and five vowels, each of which can be uttered in two different ways, either long or short; of course, some of them have different and more simple original sounds. For another example, Japanese letters will be taken which are not real simple consonants, such as those in English, but the five vowels also are real simple original sounds. All of the Japanese consonants have compound sounds with one of the vowels, so their number is just seventy-five. But if we analyze them for real simple original sounds it will be easily found that there are twenty simple original sounds, the five vowels being taken together. Consequently, the following definition can be given:

I. Every language consists of simple and original sounds which are the same throughout the world.

II. The simple original sounds are not over fifty at the most.

III. The difference of the languages comes only from the difference of the arrangement and combination of the series of the simple original sounds. For this reason, if any language is analyzed for its simple original sounds, the uniformity will be found which is the foundation of the special rules for transforming unfamiliar languages. In many cases a series of two or three simple original sounds will have a general similarity in all the languages of the world, and sometimes a series of more than three single original sounds will have the same similarity, and, therefore, while a series of certain single original sounds may correspond to one word in one language it may be a syllable in another. Accordingly, a series of some single original sounds of a language which is not familiar to us will be made to coincide with it, applying transformation by the analogous sound.

§ 2.—Transformation and Association.

In order to memorize at the same time both the pronunciation and the meaning of an unfamiliar foreign word two associations must be formed. The first association is formed of two or more words transformed from one foreign word, and the second between the first association and the meaning of the original word. Thus, forming two associations, a recollection of the pronunciation instantly recalls the meaning, and that of the meaning recalls the pronunciation. Therefore the following three courses will always be followed:

1. Transformation of unfamiliar foreign languages.
2. Association between transformed words from one original word.
3. Association between the preceding association and the meaning of the original foreign language.

If for transforming one unknown foreign word only one familiar word is applied, the second of the preceding three courses will be discarded from the practical application.

A. TRANSFORMATION OF JAPANESE LANGUAGE.

TABLE VIII.

Original word	ichi.	ni.	san.	shi.	go.	roku.
Transformed word	*itch.*	*knee.*	*sun.*	*sea.*	*gold.*	*rock.*
Meaning	one.	two.	three.	four.	five.	six.
Original word	shichi.	hachi.	ku.	ju.		
Transformed word	*sea chick.*	*hatchet.*	*cool.*	*Jew.*		
Meaning	seven.	eight.	nine.	ten.		

B. ASSOCIATION.

(Of Table VIII.)

(Itch—one)   The *itch* is not good for *one*.
(Knee—two)   The *knees* are *two* in number.
(Sun—three)   The *sun* shines some *days*.
(Sea—four)   A *foe* escaped over the *sea*.
(Gold—five)   Some *gold* to buy *cakes*.
(Rock—six)   The *rocks* are small in their *size*.
(Sea-chick—seven)   I have seen a *sea-chick seven* times.
(Hatchet—eight)   A *hatchet* injured an *aged* man.
(Cool—nine)   *Cool* water is good for an injured *knee*.
(Jew—ten)   A *Jew* bought some beer.

(*Vide ut supra* for the transformed words of numerals.)

(Of Table IX.)

1. (Mizzle—water)   *Mizzle* is also *water*.
2. (Some, sack—cold)   I took *some sacks* on a *cold* day.
3. (Sea, moss—frost)   *Frost* whitened the *seashore* covered by *moss*.
4. (Ewe, key—snow)   A *ewe* and *key* lost in the *snow*.
5. (Tomb of Dutch—friend)   I went with my *friend* to look at a *tomb* of the *Dutch*.
6. (Catarrh—shoulder)   I have *catarrh* in the *shoulder*.
7. (Key, oar, die—brother)   My *brother* saw a man in the water with a *key* and an *oar* in his hand who was about to *die*.

TABLE IX.

Number	Original words	Transformed words	Meaning
1	midzu.	*mizzle.*	water.
2	samusa.	*some sack.*	cold.
3	shimo.	*sea moss.*	frost.
4	yuki.	*ewe key.*	snow.
5	tomodachi.	*tomb of Dutch.*	friend.
6	kata.	*catarrh.*	shoulder.

Number	Original words	Transformed words	Meaning
7	kiodai.	*key our die.*	brother.
8	kao.	*cow.*	face.
9	Kuchi.	*cool cheese.*	mouth.
10	shiro.	*sea row.*	white.
11	midori.	*middling.*	green.
12	ye.	*yesterday.*	picture.

Number	Original words	Transformed words	Meaning
13	miyako.	*mist aconite.*	capital.
14	biyo in.	*bee ointment.*	hospital.
15	ginko.	*gimlet cold.*	bank.
16	shibai.	*sea bag.*	theatre.
17	mado.	*mud.*	window.
18	ame.	*amen.*	rain.

Number	Original words	Transformed words	Meaning
19	matsuribi.	*mats levee.*	holiday.
20	hiraku.	*hillock.*	open.
21	tsukue.	*cents quest.*	desk.
22	sumi.	*smith.*	ink.
23	ni kai.	*knee kite.*	up-stairs.
24	yu han.	*ewe hand.*	supper.

Number	Original words	Transformed words	Meaning
25	bun ten.	*boon ten.*	grammar.
26	reki shi.	*lake sea.*	history.
27	su gaku.	*suit gargle.*	mathematics.
28	chi.	*cheat.*	blood.
29	shin kio.	*shoe key owner.*	religion.
30	tera.	*terra.*	church.

MNEMONICS

8	(Cow—face)	*Face* of *cow*.
9	(Cool, cheese—mouth)	A *cool cheese* in the *mouth* of a jar.
10.	(Sea, row—white)	*Sea rowing* is dangerous because of *white* caps
11	(Middling—green)	The *middling* shade of *green*.
12.	(Yesterday—picture)	A *picture* was bought *yesterday*
13	(Mist, aconite—capital)	I went to *capital* on a *misty* day and bought *aconite*
14	(Bee, ointment—hospital)	A *hospital* having some sick persons stung by a *bee* prepared a great deal of *ointment*
15.	(Gimlet—cold, bank)	I went to the *bank* to get money to buy a *gimlet* on a very *cold* day
16	(She, buy—theatre)	*She* went to *buy* a *theatre*.
17	(Mud—window)	The *window* was spoiled by *mud*.
18	(Amen—rain)	An insane man said *amen* in the *rain*
19	(Mats, levee—holiday)	On a *holiday mats* were prepared to use at a *levee*.
20	(Hillock—open)	In the *open* day a *hillock* was seen.
21	(Took, yesterday—desk)	With five cen*ts* I went in *quest* of a *desk*
22.	(Smith—ink)	I saw a *smith* buying *ink*.
23.	(Knee, kite—upstairs)	I injured my *knee* while flying a *kite up-stairs*
24	(Ewe, hand—supper)	For *supper* we had *ewe* and I cut my *hand*.
25	(Boon, ten—grammar)	A *boon* of *ten grammar* books
26	(Lake, sea—history)	That a *lake* became a *sea* is clear in *history*.
27	(Sue, gargle—mathematics)	I spoiled my *suit* making a *gargle* for a mathematician
28	(Cheat—blood)	To *cheat* is in the *blood*
29	(Shoe, key, owner—religion)	The *shoe* and *key* having no *owner* is found by a *religionist*.
30.	(Terra—church)	*Terra* cotta was used for the *church*.

N B —To the other foreign languages the same method may be applied. It is superfluous to give examples of Latin, Greek, French, German, Hebrew, Chinese, Spanish, Russian, Italian, etc

§ 3.—Analysis of the Association and Explanation.

1. Explanation of transformation of the foreign languages.
2. Explanation of the association between the transformed parts of a foreign word.
3. Explanation of the association between the preceding association and the meaning of the original word.
4. And the analyses of the associations thus formed are necessary parts of the study for training in this system. This is, however, left to the reader's self-examination, which he should conduct after the examples given in the exercise of the registering method. (Chapter I., Part II.)

§ 4.—Application of the Registering, Linking, and Composing Methods for Memorizing Foreign Languages.

When it is necessary to memorize numerous foreign words at one time the author's experience shows that the registering method is most applicable. That is, when only the pronunciations of many words are required to be memorized, the associations formed between the transformed parts of each word should be registered one after another. When both pronunciations and meanings of many words are required to be memorized there are two methods: one is to associate the meaning of the word with the association formed between the transformed parts of each word, and then to register either the former or the latter; the other method is to register the latter into the first word of the register and the former into the second word of the register, thus removing the possibility of mistaking the order of the pronunciation and meaning. The foreign words may, of course, be memorized by the linking and composing methods, but in the author's experience the registering method is found to be most convenient.

The foreign sentence may be memorized by the same method as the English sentence. This method is explained in the next chapter, and to it the readers are referred. The applications of the registering, linking, and composing methods are omitted for the readers' self-exercise.

CHAPTER III.

MEMORIZING SENTENCES, INCLUDING SPEECH AND LECTURE.

A SENTENCE (including speech and lecture) is an expression of some facts or thoughts by a series having a certain length, formed by the connection of a certain number of simple, connected, or disconnected words. As it is clear enough that the sentence, however long it may be, includes none but simple, connected, or disconnected words, there is no doubt that a longer sentence may be individually memorized in the same manner as in memorizing words. But to memorize each part of a paragraph which consists of hundreds or thousands of these words without any omissions, regardless of their importance, is great labor and of little effect. It is enough to memorize the most important parts of a sentence, and there exists no necessity to memorize each part. The present method cannot be adopted for memorizing all the words of a sentence, but it presents a most practical method by which each important part of a long sentence or speech is caught and associated as it is heard or seen. There is, however, an exception. As the sentences by famous authors are excellent in their every word, these furnish models for the beginner, and the purpose of memorizing such sentences may often be different from that of memorizing a common sentence.

The memorizer may want to preserve them in his brain and recite them as he is required for the benefit of his friends. To memorize them is to memorize the whole word, not to memorize their essentials only. For such sentences several methods are adopted to memorize their whole word individually. In the following explanation the former class of sentences is called the first class and the latter the second class.

§ 1.—Rules.

I. The sentences of the first class may be memorized by catching some important parts, selected by representing transformation, which one thinks to be comprehensive enough to represent the significance of certain parts of the sentence.

II. The sentence of the second class may be memorized, first, by extracting the first words of each section and by associating them into a register, and secondly by associating the whole words in each section by the linking or composing methods, or by reciting one phrase after another in each section.

III. The register to be used under the present method may more conveniently be taken from the titles given to the sentence, or the name of the author, or certain words in the beginning.

§ 2.—Exercise in Memorizing Sentences.

A. OF THE FIRST CLASS

The method of memorizing speeches and lectures is just the same as for memorizing sentences of the first class, therefore the same process is applied to them. Here an example of sentences is given. The reader may improvise other kinds of sentences.

1. Example

1. Sentences to be Memorized.

"The grief that universally pervaded all classes at Missolonghi on the announcement of his death would be as difficult as superfluous to describe. No honor that could be devised was too great to be lavished on his remains. At Salona, where the Congress had assembled, his soul was prayed for in the church; after which the whole garrison and the citizens went out into the plain, where another religious ceremony took place under the shade of the olive-trees. This being concluded, the troops fired, and an oration, full of the warmest praise and gratitude, was pronounced by the High Priest." (A paragraph in the "Life of Lord Byron.")

2. Method to be Applied

In memorizing sentences the registering method is most convenient to be adopted, in the author's experience. The example given above is not very long, so a register consisting of fifteen words seems to be sufficient, as follows:

3. Register

a, b, c, d, e, f, g, h, i, j, k, l, m, n, o.

4. Association

1. *Ape* having a great *grief* on the *death* of its offspring } First sentence
2. *Beans* with the grease (Greece)

3. *Ceiling* was made by an artist of great *honor* } Second sentence.
4. *Deer's dead baby* was found

5. *Ear* of *saloon* keeper was hurt } Third sentence
6. *Fox* don't listen to *prayer*.

7. *Gin* is liked by *soldiers*
8. *Hat* fashioned among *citizens*
9. *Iron* mine discovered in a *plain* } Fourth sentence.
10. *No joke* in the *religious ceremony*
11. *Kittens* playing in *the shade of olive-trees*.

12 *Lion* in dread of *troops*
13 A *man fired* a gun.
14. *Name* of one who made an *excellent oration* is not unknown
15 Overcoat worn by a *High Priest*

} Fifth sentence.

5. Abridged Explanation of the Association of Ideas

1 The phrase, "The grief that universally pervaded all classes on announcement of his death was such as is difficult to describe," is represented by a connected word, "great grief on death," under the rule of transformation by different words

2 The subject of the grief being "Missolonghi,"—that is, Greece,—it is transformed into "grease" by representing by different words

3 The phrase, "No honor that could be devised was too great to be lavished on" is represented by a different word, "greatest honor."

4 The subject of the honor being "his remains," it is represented by a different word, "dead body "

5 "Salona" is transformed into "saloon" by changing transformation.

6 The word "prayer" is extracted to represent the phrase, "his soul was prayed for in the church "

7. " Garrison" is transformed into a different word, "soldier."

8. "Citizens" has no transformation.

9. "Plain" has no transformation

10. "Religious ceremony" has no transformation.

11 "Shade of olive-trees" has no transformation These five simple words extracted, "soldier," "citizen," "plain," and "religious ceremony," and a combined word, "shade of olive-trees," represent the phrase, "after which the whole garrison and citizens went out to the plain, where another religious ceremony took place under the shade of the olive-trees "

12 "Troops" has no transformation

13 "Fired" has no transformation. These two words extracted represent the phrase, "This being concluded, the troops fired."

14 The phrase, "an oration, full of the warmest praise and gratitude," is represented by a combined word, ' excellent oration "

15 "High priest" has no transformation The two words extracted represent the phrase, "an oration, full of the warmest praise and gratitude, was pronounced by the High Priest "

2. Example.

1. Sentence to be Memorized.

"The fireplaces were of a truly patriarchal magnitude, where the whole family, old and young, master and servant, black and white,—nay, even the very cat and dog,—enjoyed a community of privilege and had each a right to a corner. Here the old burgher would sit in perfect silence puffing his pipe, looking in the fire with half-shut eyes, and thinking of nothing for hours together; the good wife, on the opposite side, would employ herself diligently in spinning yarn or knitting stockings. The young folks would crowd around the hearth, listening with breathless attention to some old crone of a negro, who was the oracle of the family, and who, perched like a raven in a corner of the chimney, would croak forth for a long winter afternoon a string of incredible stories about New England witches, grisly ghosts, horses without heads, hairbreadth escapes, and bloody encounters among Indians" ("Knickerbocker's History of New York," by Washington Irving.)

2. Selection of a Register

A register which has some relation to the sentence is preferred, as follows:

k, n, i, c, k, e, r, b, o, c, k, e, r, h, i, s, t, o, r, y

N.B.—As has already been explained under the chapter on registering method, the perfect register should be such as does not include two identical words. When it is decided to adopt an imperfect register, however, as given above, it must be borne in mind to transform the two identical words in a way by which it may be clearly recollected that one was first in order and the other next. For instance, first "k" may be transformed into "kitchen," second "k" into "kite," and the third "k" into "kitten." In these transformations it is clear, from the alphabetical arrangement, that "kitchen" precedes "kite," and "kite" precedes "kitten."

3 Associations.

1. I made a *great fireplace* in the *kitchen*.
2. The *whole family* are *nice*.
3. *Idle men enjoy* nothing
4. A *burgher* was buying *cane*.
5. He was flying a *kite* in *perfect silence*.
6. *Tobacco* cannot be *eaten*.
7. She *thinks* of *nothing* but to buy a *ring*
8. *Beautiful wife*
9. *Old* woman unable to *spin* or *knit*
10. The *young folks* wearing *caps*
11. A *kitten* plays around the *hearth*
12. *Listen* to a speech on *economy*.
13. A *room* occupied by a *negro*.
14. History contained *incredible stories*.

N.B.—Explanations of the transformations and associations are left to the reader's examination.

B. OF THE SECOND CLASS.

Example

1 Sentence to be Memorized.

"Sir, the atrocious crime of being a young man, which the honorable gentleman has with such spirit and decency charged upon me, I shall neither attempt to palliate nor deny; but content myself by wishing that I may be one of those whose follies may cease with their youth, and not of those who continue ignorant in spite of age and experience, etc" (For the whole the readers are referred to Pitt's speech in reply to Horace Walpole.)

The main significance of the above famous speech may be thus divided:

First paragraph explains that he was reproached as being a youth.

Second paragraph explains that an aged man may be worse than a youth.

Third paragraph explains that he was again reproached with acting a theatrical part.

Fourth paragraph explains that he is free to use his own language.

Fifth paragraph explains that a charge was made that he who utters any sentiments but his own commits a great offence.

Sixth paragraph explains that the act which offended them is his zeal for the service of the country.

2 SELECTION OF THE REGISTER

The famous sentences having a title may be most conveniently memorized by selecting the title or name of the author as a register, for by so doing the recollection of impressions is very easily made. The author of the present system has memorized more than seventy famous compositions, as described in "The Models of the Chinese Composition," without failing in a word. The registers adopted in this case were all the title or author's name of the composition. In the present instance the title is selected for the register, as follows:

Register —Pitt in reply to Horace Walpole.

3. TRANSFORMATION AND REGISTRATION

1 "Youth" is extracted from the first paragraph to represent the whole The register "Pitt" is transformed into "spit." "There is a youth who used to spit" (Registration)

2. "Aged man" and "worse" are extracted from the second paragraph The register is transformed into "ink." "An aged man bought worse ink." (Registration)

3 "Theatre" is extracted from the third paragraph. "I must write a reply to an invitation to the theatre " (Registration)

4 "Free" is extracted from the fourth paragraph. The register "to" is transformed into "token." "The freedom is a token of civilization." (Registration.)

5 " A charge for borrowed opinion" and "offence" are extracted from the fifth paragraph The register "Horace" is transformed into "horse." " I met a man on horseback who made a charge for borrowed opinion to others and was sued for the offence." (Registration)

4 Linking.

By the above registered associations the main significance of the speech is all memorized. Now we must associate each phrase in detail by the linking method.

1 ("Sir" with "the atrocious crime ") Circumstantial evidence of an atrocious crime

2 ("Atrocious crime" with "young man ") Atrocious crime was committed by a young man

3 ("Young man" with "the honorable gentleman ') The young man may become an honorable gentleman

4 ("Honorable gentleman" with "spirit and decency ") Man cannot become an honorable gentleman without spirit and decency

5 ("Spirit and decency" with "charged ") Spirit and decency is not charged by anyone.

6 ("Charged" with " palliate or deny ") One who is charged must palliate or deny

7 (" Palliate or deny" with "content ") If he succeeds in the effort to palliate or deny he must be contented

8 ("Content" with " wishing ") A contented man wishes for nothing

9 ("Wishing" with "follies ") I don't wish to be a victim of follies

10 ("Follies" with "cease with youth ") The follies cease with youth

11. ("Cease with youth" with "no wish ") There is rarely a youth who has no wish

12. ("No wish" with "continue ignorant ") I have no wish to continue ignorant.

13 ("Continue ignorant" with "age and experience.") Ignorance ceases with age and experience.

N.B —The readers must be very careful to understand the application of the rules of transformation

CHAPTER IV.

MEMORIZING POETICAL COMPOSITION.

The poem, from its nature, must be memorized word for word, and has not much interest if merely the essence is memorized, like the sentence of the first kind. It is almost the same as the sentence of the second kind, and thus the way by which it is memorized resembles the process that is pursued in memorizing the latter.

§ 1.—Rules for Memorizing Poetical Compositions.

I. Each word composing a verse should be associated by the linking or composing methods.

II. Next, each verse should be associated by the linking or composing methods.

III. If the registering method only is applied, each verse should be divided into each word and registered.

IV. One or two words may be extracted from a verse, to represent the whole, and registered.

§ 2.—Exercise in Memorizing Poetical Composition.

A. APPLICATION OF THE LINKING METHOD.

Example

1. Poem to be Memorized

"Twinkle, twinkle, little star,
How I wonder what you are,
Up above the world so high,
Like a diamond in the sky!"

MEMORIZING POETICAL COMPOSITION. 143

2 Linking

1. ("Twinkle" with "twinkle") "Twinkle" and "twinkle" are identical
2. ("Twinkle" with "little star") A twinkling little star.
3. ("Star" with "how I wonder") A star fell, and how I wondered
4. ("Wonder" with "what you are") I wonder, when asked by a man, what you are.
5. ("What you are" with "up above the world") We cannot know exactly what there is up above the world
6. ("World" with "so high") A word was uttered so high
7. ("High" with "like a diamond") In the high mountain I found a stone like a diamond
8. ("Diamond" with "in the sky") Diamonds do not rain from the sky

B APPLICATION OF THE REGISTERING METHOD.

Examples.

1 Poem to be Memorized.

"Hear the sledges with their bells—
    Silver bells!
What a world of merriment their melody foretells!
    How they tinkle, tinkle, tinkle,
      In the icy air of night!
    While the stars that over sprinkle
    All the heavens seem to twinkle
      With a crystalline delight,
    Keeping time, time, time,
    In a sort of Runic rhyme,
To the tintinnabulation that so musically wells
From the bells, bells, bells, bells, bells, bells—
From the jingling and the tinkling of the bells"

2 Selection of Register.

If each verse of the above poem be divided into simple or connected words less than five, a register consisting of fourteen groups, each group having five parts, may suffice, as follows:

Ba, be, bi, bo, bu.
Ca, ce, ci, co, cu,
Da, de, di, do, du
Fa, fe, fi, fo, fu
Ga, ge, gi, go, gu
Ha, he, hi, ho, hu.
Ja, je, ji, jo, ju,

Ka, ke, ki, ko, ku.
La, le, li, lo, lu.
Ma, me, mi, mo, mu.
Na, ne, ni, no, nu
Pa, pe, pi, po, pu.
Qa, qe, qi, qo, qu
Ra, re, ri, ro, ru.

3. Registration

1		1 (Ba—hear)	Baby hears the parent's voice.
		2 (Be—the sledge with the bells)	Drinking beer on the sledges with the bells
2.		3 (Ca—the silver bells)	A car with silver bells
3		4 (Da—what a world of merriment)	Dancing is a world of merriment.
		5 (De—their melody)	Dentist bought bells and examined their melody.
		6 (Di—foretells)	A diplomat foretells eternal peace
4		7 (Fa—how they)	A fat man does not pay housage
		8 (Fe—tinkle, tinkle, tinkle)	A felon was disturbed by many disturbing tinklings (Disturbing represents three, and may indicate three times. Refer to "Memorizing Numerals.")
5		9 (Ga—in the icy air of night)	Gate was broken in the icy air of night

MEMORIZING POETICAL COMPOSITION. 145

6	10 (Ha—while)	White hat
	11. (He—the stars that over sprinkle)	Over the head there are the stars that over sprinkle.
7	12 (Ja—all the heavens)	By jackets we cannot cover all the heavens
	13 (Je—seem to twinkle)	All jewels seem to twinkle
8	14. (Ka—with a crystalline)	A kangaroo frightened by a crystal.
	15. (Ke—delight)	I am delighted to get a foreign kettle.
9	16 (La—keeping)	A lantern keeping light in a cell.
	17 (Le—time, time, time)	Alexander surviving many dangerous times
10	18 (Ma—in a sort of Runic rhyme)	A mastering song is a sort of Runic rhyme.
11	19. (Na—to the tintinnabulation that so musically wells)	Nails in box ring to the tintinnabulation that so musically wells in moving them
	20 (Ne—wells)	Needle found in the well
12	21 (Pa—from)	A form made by paper
	22. (Pe—bells, bells, bells, bells)	A peasant keeps many fine bells. (Fine represents four, and may indicate four times)
13	23 (Qua—bells, bells, bells)	A quack doctor bought many dirty bells (Dirty represents three)
14	24 (Ra—from the jingling and the tinkling of the bells)	All the rats in the house ran away from the jingling and tinkling of the bells

C. APPLICATION OF COMPOSING METHOD.

Example

1. Poem to be Memorized

" Be the matter what it may,
Always speak the truth.
If at work or if at play,
Always speak the truth "

2 Composition.

"In the dining-room a *bee* stung my *mother*. I ran away and, leaving my *hat*, stopped to *eat*. I then went into the garden where there were *many* flower-blossoms, and thought about *all ways* to excuse myself I found there my father, and hurried to *speak the truth*, who told me that *if at work* or *if at play* I must *always speak the truth* about every trifling matter"

CHAPTER V.

MEMORIZING NAMES.

MEN's names may be classified into two kinds: the one is familiar and the other is unfamiliar. The former is a simple or connected word and the latter a disconnected word. These principles have already been explained in Part I., and the several exercises taking unfamiliar names treated them as disconnected words of the second class. Names are such important subjects of memorization in the daily life that they cannot be left to the routine concerning the disconnected words of the second class. They require some easy method by which they can be instantly memorized. For these reasons the following rules are given:

§ 1.—Rules Relating to the Names.

The kinds of the second names that are commonly adopted are limited, while the persons who adopt them are unlimited. Hence there are many persons who have the same second name. Among them there often may be one whom you know of personally or are acquainted with in history. Thus, when a name is required to be memorized, you should first search for the person having the same second name with whom you are personally acquainted or know of in history. If you succeed in your search, the name required to be memorized should be transformed into the name of the person already known, by which a person's name required to be memorized becomes transformed into a familiar name, and is thus easily and firmly impressed upon the mind. This method is one instance of transformation by identical sound. If you do not find any acquaintance having the same name you should transform it into the only familiar name. When these two methods fail it must be transformed by the same means as are disconnected words of the second kind, which process has already been explained. The first name may also be memorized in the same manner. If you have an intimate friend or relative who has the same first name as that required to be memorized, and whom you habitually called by the first name, without referring to the second name, you may adopt the same method as above explained, thus transforming the name of the person with whom you are unacquainted into the name of your friend or relative. If you fail to find such friend or relative having the same first name, you should search for acquainted or known persons whose second name is the same as the first name required to be memorized. And lastly, if you fail in this, you should transform the first name in hand into the second familiar name, as Charles into Charlemagne. If these three methods fail, the first name should be transformed by the method adaptable to disconnected words of the second kind.

§ 2.—Exercise in Memorizing Names.

Examples.

1. Names to be Memorized.

1. James Grant	4 Frank Thomas	7. Richard Booth
2. George Cromwell.	5 Francis Tenny.	8 William Greenleaf.
3 Edward Peet	6. Charles Anderson	9. John Markly

2 Transformation

1. Original words	James	Grant
Transformed words	James (second name of friend)	Grant (American general)
2 Original words	George	Cromwell
Transformed words	George (first name of brother)	Cromwell (Oliver Cromwell)

MEMORIZING NAMES 149

3	Original words	. Edward	Peet.
	Transformed words	Edward (Edward the Confessor)	Pitt (Lord Chatham).
4	Original words	Frank	Thomas
	Transformed words	Franklin (discoverer of electricity)	Thompson (American electrician).
5	Original words	Francis	Tenny.
	Transformed words	Francis (French king)	Tennyson (poet)
6	Original words	. Charles	Anderson
	Transformed words	. Charlemagne (the great king)	Anderson (actress).
7.	Original words	. Richard	Booth
	Transformed words	. Richard (Shakespeare's)	Booth (actor)
8.	Original words	William	Greenleaf
	Transformed words	. William (baby of neighbor)	Greenleaf (author of law)
9	Original words	. John	Markly
	Transformed words	John (of Magna Charta)	Macbeth (Shakespeare's)

3. Association.

The names may be memorized by either method The registering and composing methods severally or jointly may be most conveniently applied. The readers are required to form their own association It is here sufficient to give an example of transformation

CHAPTER VI.

MEMORIZING UNFAMILIAR OR UNKNOWN THINGS AND EVENTS OR FACTS AND CONNECTION OF THE NAMES WITH THEM.

§ 1.—Kind of Things and Events Unknown.

1. Person unknown.
2. Birds, quadrupeds, and fish unknown.
3. Grasses and trees unknown.
4. Metals and stones unknown.
5. Tools unknown.
6. Astronomical and geographical objects unknown.
7. Words and letters unknown.
8. Events unknown.

N B —The person unknown (1) includes one who is a stranger and whose name is unknown, or one whose person is known but whose name is unknown, or one whose name is known but whose person is unknown

§ 2.—Special Rules for Transformation.

The rules explained in Parts I. and II. are, of course, adaptable for the transformation of unknown objects or facts. But there are some special rules applicable to the purpose by which the unknown objects or facts are transformed into certain familiar words, so as to be susceptible to the operation of the methods explained in Part II. They are as follows:

I. Representation by Selection.

Representation by selection, like the representation by selected words (one of transformations), is to extract some prominent feature out of character, quality, form, position, sound, color, action, smell, or other peculiarity of the unknown objects or facts, and to let the words representing the prominent feature represent the whole object or part. For instance, in a man having macula, or having one eye, it is required to memorize the prominent feature; that is, macula and one eye should be selected, and the words macula and one eye, indicating the feature, will represent the man

II Representation by Identification

Representation by identification, like transformation by identical sounds, is to find out some feature in the character, quality, form, position, sound, color, action, smell, or other peculiarities of the unknown objects or facts which is identical to that of known objects or facts, and to make the words indicating the known objects or facts represent the unknown ones Thus in a case when the nature of crystal is to be memorized, and it is found that its transparency is the same as that of glass, the word glass is borrowed to represent the crystal

III Representation by Analogy

Representation by analogy, like transformation by analogous sound, is to represent the unknown objects or facts by words indicating the familiar objects or facts which are analogous to the unknown ones Thus, in the case of memorizing a tree, whose leaves have the shape of beans, the word beans represents the tree.

IV. Representation by Position

Representation by position is to represent the unknown objects or facts by the words indicating the place or position where they were found or appeared Thus, in memorizing Fuji Mountain, the name of the country in which it is, that is, Japan, is to represent it

V Representation by Attributing

Representation by attributing is, when any feature explained in the above four rules cannot be found, to attribute according to one's own idea the unknown objects or facts, and to represent them by the attributing words Thus, in memorizing an unknown person you may characterize his face as smiling, and use the word smiling to represent the person.

§ 3.—Transformation of Unknown Things or Facts into Words.

A. TRANSFORMATION OF UNKNOWN PERSONS INTO WORDS

In transforming unknown persons into words, according to the transforming rules (§ 2) we notice two kinds of persons, as follows:

I. TRANSFORMATION OF THE UNKNOWN PERSONS IN WHOM SPECIAL FEATURES CAN EASILY BE FOUND

1. Examples.

1. One who has pock-marks on his face.
2. One whose hairs are all white
3. One whose body is very fat
4. One whose complexion resembles that of Napoleon Bonaparte.
5. One who is very short.
6. One having a bald head.
7. One having a thick beard.
8. One who always has a gloomy expression.
9. One who is not normal in speaking.
10. One whose backbone is bent forward

2. Transformation.

1. He is represented by the words pock-marks
2. He is represented by the words white hairs
3. He is represented by the words fat body
4. He is represented by the words Napoleon Bonaparte.
5. He is represented by the words short body.
6. He is represented by the words bald head
7. He is represented by the words thick beard
8. He is represented by the word gloomy.
9. He is represented by the word stutterer
10. He is represented by the words round shoulders

II. TRANSFORMATION OF PERSONS IN WHOM SPECIAL FEATURES CANNOT EASILY BE FOUND

Practically we find very few persons who have, apparently, the special features adaptable to the rules explained in § 2. Thus, to complete the system of memorizing the complexion, it is necessary to make the rules by which whatever face is met may instantly be transformed into a representing word. The author after hard study established a rule by which whenever one complexion or feature is found insufficient to represent the person, more than two complexions or features (as many as it is thought sufficient to represent) are selected, and they are again concentrated into one representing word, *i.e.*, a connected word. This is called the selecting and concentrating method.

1. Sphere of Application of the Selecting and Concentrating Method.

A Form of Face

The form of the face is classified into six kinds:

1 Round face
2 Square face
3. Long face
4. Middle face.
5 High-cheek face.
6. Short face

B. Color of Face.

The color of the face is classified into five kinds:

1 White.
2 Dark.
3. Red
4 Pale.
5 Yellow.

C Profile of Face

The profile of the face is classified into nine kinds:

1 Hollowed
2. Convexed
3 Plane
4. Fat
5. Thin
6 Large
7 Small
8 Long
9 Short

D Expression.

The expression of the face is classified into eleven kinds:

1. Gloomy expression
2. Agreeable expression.
3. Sober expression
4. Gentle expression
5. Disagreeable expression.
6. Happy expression
7. Poor expression
8. Wicked expression
9. Wise expression
10. Foolish expression.
11. Sulky expression

2. Formation of Concentrated Word (Connected Word).

If one of the above features is thought sufficient to represent, there is no necessity for the applying, selecting, and concentrating methods. But in the contrary case two, three, or more features must be selected as far as it is thought sufficient to represent, and they must all be concentrated. The formation of concentrated words is not very easy work, and must be previously prepared by each individual. The manner in which they are formed is to take the form of face as the principal element, and by associating other features with it to form a connected word. For instance, one who has a square face of dark color is represented by a connected word, dark square. One who has a square face of plain profile is represented by a connected word, plain square. One who has a square face of gloomy expression is represented by a connected word, gloomy square. The concentrated words are always formed by two features. When it is thought that one concentrated word is not enough to represent, the concentrated word should be associated with one or more features by the composing method, so as to form a connected word which will represent the person. The concentrated words formed by the author are of three kinds, as follows:

MEMORIZING UNFAMILIAR OBJECTS. 155

a. The Concentrated Words of the First Kind. (Form and Color of Face.)

Color		white.	dark.	red.	pale.	yellow.
Form—Round face		white ground.	dark ground.	round lead.	round pall.	yellow ground.
Square face		white squirrel.	dark squirrel.	red squirrel.	square pall.	yellow square.
Long face		long kite.	long dirk.	long lead.	long pail.	long willow.
Middle face		middle kite.	middle dirk.	red fiddle.	middle pall.	middle willow.
High-cheek face		white cheese.	cheap dirk.	red cheek.	pale cheek.	yellow cheese.
Short face		white shirt.	dark shirt.	red shirt.	short pall.	short willow.

b. The Concentrated Words of the Second Kind. (Form and Profile of Face.)

Profile		hollowed.	convexed.	plane.	fat.	thin.	large.	small.	long.	short.
Form—Round face	{	hollowed ground.	convexed ground.	plane ground.	round hat.	round thing.	large ground.	small ground.	—	—
Square face	{	square hollow.	convexed square.	plane square.	square hat.	square thing.	large square.	small square.	—	short square.
Long face	{	long hollowness.	long convex.	long plane.	long hat.	long thing.	large tongue.	small tongue.	—	—
Middle face	{	middle hollowness.	middle convex.	middle plane.	middle hat.	middle thing.	large fiddle.	small fiddle.	long cheek.	—
High-cheek face	{	hollowed cheek.	convexed cheek.	plane cheek.	cheap hat.	cheap thing.	large cheek.	small cheek.	long cheese.	short cheese.
Short face	{	short hollowness.	short convict.	short plane.	short hat.	short thing.	—	—	—	—

N. B.—The short lines indicate that no such cases exist.

MNEMONICS.

c. The Concentrated Words of the Third Kind. (Form and Expression of Face.)

Expression	gloomy.	agreeable.	sober.	gentle.	disagreeable.	happy.	poor.	wicked.	wise.	foolish.	sulky.
Form—Round face {	gloomy ground.	agreeable ground.	sober sound.	gentle sound.	disagreeable ground.	happy ground.	poor ground.	sound wicked man.	sound wise man.	foolish sound.	round sulky.
Square face {	gloomy square.	agreeable square.	sober squirrel.	square gentleman.	disagreeable square.	happy square.	poor square.	wicked squirrel.	wise squirrel.	foolish squirrel.	square sulky.
Long face ... {	long gloom.	long agreement.	sober tongue.	gentle tongue.	disagreeable tongue.	happy song.	poor song.	wicked song.	wise song.	foolish song.	sulky song.
Middle face .. {	middle gloom.	agreeable fiddle.	middle sofa.	gentle fiddle.	disagreeable fiddle.	happy fiddle.	poor fiddle.	wicked fiddle.	wise riddle.	foolish riddle.	middle sulky.
High-cheek face {	cheap loom.	agreeable cheese.	sober cheater.	gentle cheater.	disagreeable cheese.	cheap hop.	poor cheese.	wicked cheese.	cheerful wise man.	cheerful fool.	cheap sulky.
Short face ... {	short gloom.	agreeable shirt.	sober sport.	short gentleman.	disagreeable shirt.	happy sport.	poor shirt.	wicked sport.	wise sport.	foolish sport.	sulky sport.

MEMORIZING UNFAMILIAR OBJECTS.

Exercise for Selection and Concentration.

1 Example

1. One having square face of white color
2. One having round face of gentle expression
3. One having long and thin face
4. One having middle face of dark color
5. One having convexed and short face
6. One having high cheek and wise expression
7. One having pale and agreeable complexion
8. One having hollow square face of white color
9. One having red, long face with wicked expression
10. One having disagreeable long face of white color and high cheek.

2 Concentration.

1 The person is represented by the concentrated word "white squirrel" or "square kite"

2 The person is represented by the concentrated word "sound gentleman" or "gentle sound"

3 The person is represented by the concentrated word "long thing" or "thin tongue"

4. The person is represented by the concentrated word "middle park" or "dirk"

5 The person is represented by the concentrated word "short convex"

6 The person is represented by the concentrated word "wise cheater"

7 The person is represented by the concentrated word "agreeable pail"

8 The person is represented by the concentrated word "white squirrel in hollow"

9 The person is represented by the concentrated word 'wicked song is read."

10 The person is represented by the concentrated word "cheap kite was bought by a man singing a disagreeable song"

B. TRANSFORMATION OF UNKNOWN BIRDS, QUADRUPEDS, INSECTS, AND FISH INTO WORDS

When unknown birds, quadrupeds, insects, and fish are required to be memorized the most eminent features in their shape, color of feather or scales, the position of each organ, place of living, their voice, and the kind of movements should be selected to represent the objects. If it is considered insufficient for the purpose of representation to select one feature, other features should be selected and concentrated, as in the former cases.

Examples.

1. THE OBJECTS TO BE MEMORIZED.

1. A bird whose whole body is white
2. A fish whose head looks like a bald head
3. A fish whose one side is black
4. A fish whose shape is like a sword
5. A fish of blue color whose shape resembles a swallow.
6. An insect whose body is covered by fine hairs
7. An insect which makes a sound like knocking.
8. An insect which has a nature easily excited
9. An insect of black color having many feet.
10. An insect whose body is encircled by close rings

2 SELECTION AND CONCENTRATION.

1. The object is represented by a simple word, white
2. The object is represented by a connected word, bald head.
3. The object is represented by a connected word, half black.
4. The object is represented by a simple word, sword
5. The object is represented by a connected word, blue swallow.
6. The object is represented by a connected word, fine hairs
7. The object is represented by a simple word, knocking.
8. The object is represented by a simple word, excited
9. The object is represented by a connected word, black feet.
10. The object is represented by a connected word, linked rings.

C TRANSFORMATION OF UNKNOWN GRASSES, TREES, METALS, STONES, AND TOOLS INTO WORDS

I. To transform unknown grasses and trees into words, the prominent feature in the color, shape, nature, use, and odor of their branches, leaves, trunks, stems, roots, barks, flowers, or fruits should be selected, and by the word indicating the selected part they should be represented. When in selecting one feature is found insufficient, other features may be added and concentrated.

II. To transform unknown metals and stones into words, the prominent feature in their shape, color, nature, use, and place where they are found should be selected, and by the word indicating the selected feature they should be represented. When the selection of one feature is found insufficient, other features may be added and concentrated.

III. To transform unknown tools, such as are newly invented, the prominent feature in their shape, color, use, and quality should be selected, and by the word indicating the selected feature they should be represented. When extraction of one feature is found insufficient, other features may be added and concentrated.

N B.—Examples and their selection and concentration are almost similar to those given in the preceding examples.

D TRANSFORMATION OF UNKNOWN STARS, MOUNTAINS, RIVERS, CITIES, VILLAGES, AND ISLANDS INTO WORDS.

The prominent feature (1) as to the stars is their position, distance; (2) as to the mountains and rivers, their shape, height and size, length, and trees, rocks, waterfalls, cities, bridges, ships, and ferries belonging to them; (3) as to the cities, their shape, position, prosperity, number of residents, and principal buildings; (4) as to the villages, their position, number of houses, and some part of their scenery; (5) as to the islands, their shape, size, and trees should be selected, and by the word indicating the selected feature they should be represented. When selection of one feature is found insufficient to represent, the other features may be added and concentrated.

N B.—Pictures and the forms of letter or word may be memorized by the same method as in substantial objects. The examples of their selection and concentration are left to the reader.

E. TRANSFORMATION OF UNKNOWN EVENTS OR FACTS INTO WORDS.

Practically there cannot be many facts unknown, but if there be some, they must be composed of many elements which are all known to us. But in the progressing world, where new events occur day after day, sometimes there may appear facts which are entirely, as a whole or in part, unknown. In such case they should be memorized by forming a representing word, according to the attributing representation (Rule IV., § 2). Examples of the transformation are deferred to the rule.

§ 4.—Application of the Registering Method for Memorizing Unknown Objects or Facts Transformed into Words.

a Examples

1 Objects to be Memorized

The examples given and transformed in § 3 (page 152) are borrowed.

MEMORIZING UNFAMILIAR OBJECTS.

2 Register

1, 2, 3, 4, 5, 6, 7, 8, 9, 10.

3. Registration

1. (1—pock-marks)   *Bee s stings* deface a man like *pock-marks*.
2. (2—white hairs)   A man with *white hairs* bought *tea*
3. (3—fat body)   One *day* I met a *fat man*
4. (4—Napoleon Bonaparte)   A *foe* owned by *Napoleon*
5. (5—short body)   *Short cake*
6. (6—bald head)   A *sea man* having a *bald head*
7. (7—thick beard)   An *ape* having a *thick beard*
8. (8—gloomy)   An *aged man* of *gloomy expression.*
9. (9—stutterer)   A *kneeling stutterer*
10. (10—round shoulders)   A *bear* having *round shoulders*

b. Examples

1 Objects to be Memorized

The examples given and transformed in § 3 (page 157) are borrowed.

2 Register

ba, be, bi, bo, bu, ca, ce, ci, co, cu

3. Registration.

1. (Ba—square kite)   A *baby* playing on a *square kite.*
2. (Be—sound gentleman)   A *bee* stung a *sound gentleman*
3. (Bi—long thing)   On a *bicycle* a *long thing* was carried
4. (Bo—middle park)   *Boys* fight in the *middle park*
5. (Bu—short convex)   *Buds* in *short convex*
6. (Ca—wise cheater)   A *wise cheater* carries *cane*
7. (Ce—agreeable pail)   In the *cellar* an *agreeable pail* is kept
8. (Ci—white squirrel in the hollow) A *white squirrel in the hollow* with *cider*
9. (Co—wicked song is read)   A *wicked song is read* by my *cousin*

11

10. (Cu—cheap kite bought by a man singing a disagreeable song)   *Cheap kite bought by a man singing a disagreeable song* was left in a field of *cucumbers*

§ 5.—Memorizing Connections of the Unknown Things and Events or Facts with their Names.

As memorizing the unknown objects or facts by a quick method is necessary, a memorization of their names at the same time is still more necessary. To give a most common instance, when we are introduced to an unknown person we may remember his appearance and not his name, or *vice versa*.

In the study of biology, mineralogy, or materia medica there are many instances where the names as well as the objects are required to be memorized. Memorizing the connection of the name with the object, however, does not need very difficult methods, but only to memorize a few rules.

a. Rules for Connection of Name with its Objects.

I. A connection is formed by associating the representative word obtained by selection or by concentration and the name of the object represented. In other words, the name of the object is taken as register to the representative word for the association.

II. When the name of the object consists of several simple words, as the name of a man, the general rule is that the principal word, the second name of the man, for instance, should be associated with the representative.

III. When a reasonable association cannot be formed between the principal name and the representative, the other part of the name should be taken in association with the representative

b. Exercise.

1. Names and Objects

The representative words are borrowed from the examples given in § 3, Chapter VI.

1. Pock-marks with James Grant.
2. White hairs with George Cromwell
3. Fat body with Edward Pitt.
4. Napoleon Bonaparte with Frank Thomas
5. Short body with Francis Tenny
6. Bald head with Charles Anderson.
7. Thick beard with Richard Booth
8. Gloomy with William Greenleaf
9. Stutter with John Markly
10. Round shoulders with Amuy Thurston

N B.—The representative of the object as given in the above example is supposed to be the eminent feature of the person

2 Association

1. One is never *glad* of *pock-marks*
2. *Cromwell* did not live until *white hair.*
3. *Fat pig*
4. *Napoleon* did not sail on the *Thames*
5. To play *tennis* for a *short time*
6. Met a man with a *bald head* in the *Andes Mountains*
7. A man of *thick beard* buying *boots*
8. When you feel *gloomy* you should look at *green leaves*
9. That *stuttering* man can *mark* things well
10. I *round* my *shoulders* to drink water, being very *thirsty*

Another Example

1 Names and Objects

The examples are borrowed of the representative words under B., § 4, Chapter VI.

1 Entirely white with stork.
2. Bald head with octopus.
3 Half black with flounder
4 Sword with trichiurus
5. Blue swallow with flying fish
6 Fine hair with caterpillar.
7 Knocking with cicada
8 Excite with mantis
9. Black feet with centiped
10. Linked rings with caterpillar

N B —The representative of objects,—that is, feature,—attributed to each fish and insect may not be true, but that is immaterial.

2 Association

1 *White stockings*
2 A man with *bald head* must protect his head since *October* has come.
3. I saw a *half-black* fish *floundering* in a net
4. There is a *treacherous* man with a *sword*
5 A fish *flying* like a *swallow*
6 Fine hairs *sticking* to a *pillow*.
7. To *knock* the *scales*
8. *Excited man* buying a *mantel*
9 A man of *black feet* buying a cent's worth of peas
10 *Linked rings* fastened to a *pillar*.

CHAPTER VII.

APPLICATION OF MNEMONICS TO THE STUDY OF SCIENCES.

THE present system may be applied to the study of any branch of science, as geography, history, physics, chemistry, law, medicine, mathematics, zoology, etc. One who studies these sciences or who is required to be examined on them can apply the system to great advantage. The special rule by which the methods are applied to these purposes will be explained in the following section.

§ 1.—Geography.

Students in geography generally complain that the size, latitude and longitude, population, kinds of the products, amount of exports and imports, heights of mountains, lengths of rivers, etc., in each country are too difficult to remember. But these facts, by the application of the present system, may be transformed into the words which are easiest to be memorized. Either method, registering, linking, or composing, may be applied, as one thinks most convenient. When the registering method is applied, however, a register must be selected which has more or less direct relation to the object required to be memorized. For instance, if 15,000 feet in reference to the Rocky Mountains be required to be memorized, the word Rocky should be taken as the register and associated with 15,000 feet.

Example

1. OBJECTS TO BE MEMORIZED.

There are twenty-three ports open to foreign trade in China. In the year 1891 the total amount of imports was 134,003,863 taels, and that of exports 100,947,849 taels.

2. TRANSFORMATION

23,	1 thousand	891,	13	4, million	0 0 3,	8 6 3.
toad	bamboo	great noble	bed,	fowl	red radish	good saddle.

	1 0 0,	million 9	4 7,	8 4 9.
	beautiful arrow	window	fop	great fan.

3. REGISTRATION.

a. Register.

a, b, c, d, e, f, g, h, i, j, k.

b. Registration

1. (A—toad)   *Ape* playing with a *toad*.
2. (B—bamboo)   I drove away *bees* with a *bamboo stick*.
3. (C—great noble)   *Cat* owned by a *great noble*.
4. (D—bed)   *Deer's bed* is the grass.
5. (E—fowl)   I like to *eat* the *fowls' flesh*.
6. (F—red radish)   *Failure* in *red radish* production.
7. (G—good saddle)   A *general* owns a *good saddle*.
8. (H—beautiful arrow)   *Hunt* with *beautiful arrows*.
9. (I—window)   *Icicle* in *window*.
10. (J—fop)   A *joking fop*.
11. (K—great fan)   A *knock* with a *great fan*.

4. COMPOSING

"There stands a man with a face like a *toad*, carrying a cane made of *bamboo*, who is a *great noble* of the country. He laid in *bed* and looked at a *fowl* which was eating *red radish* near him. He soon got up and

APPLICATION TO THE STUDY OF SCIENCES. 167

put a *good saddle* on his horse and rode, carrying a *beautiful arrow*, and in the *window* of a house he saw a *fop* with a *great fan* who was looking out"

§ 2.—History.

The matters most difficult to remember in the study of history are the periods when certain important events occurred or ceased, the dates when certain heroes were born or died, or the names of the persons who were concerned in an important event. By application of the present system, however, there is no difficulty in these matters, nor will there be in geography. The register in this case should be such as has some relation to the matters required to be memorized.

Example

1. OBJECT TO BE MEMORIZED

"About one hundred and fifty years after that event (deluge) Nimrod, the grandson of Ham, the son of Noah, built Babylon, on the river Euphrates, and Assur, the son of Shem, and grandson of Noah, built the city of Nineveh, on the river Tigris, which became the capital of the Assyrian Empire"

2 REGISTER

h, i, s, t, o, r, y, o, f, a, n, c, i, e, n, t, a, g, e.

3 REGISTRATION.

1 (H—150)   *Horse* pulling a beautiful car
2. (I—deluge)   An *idol* lost in the *deluge*
3 (S—Nimrod)   A *surgeon* was asking the *name* of a lad.
4. (T—grandson)   *Toy* bought for a *grandson*
5 (O—Ham)   *Omelet* having pieces of *ham*
6 (R—son)   A *rascal* talking with the *son*
7. (Y—Noah)   *Yes* and *no* are antagonistic
8 (O—Babylon)   An *ox* has a *baby on* his back
9. (F—Euphrates)   *Fruits* on a *few plates*

10. (A—assur)   An *ape* on *ass*
11 (N—son)   In the *night* I sing a *song*
12. (C—Shem)   *Captain* got a *shame*
13. (I—and)   *Isolated land*
14 (E—grandson)   I gave an *eagle* to my *grandson*
15. (N—Noah)   *No* and *Noah* are of analogous sound
16 (T—Nineveh)   *Nine trunks* were bought
17 (A—Tigris)   *Arm* at a *tiger.*
18 (G—Assyria)   A *great asylum.*

§ 3.—Law.

In the study of law, especially of codified law, there are very many items to be memorized, and it is almost impossible to do it. By application of the present system, however, we can do it without using the least labor. The way by which law is memorized is not very different from the process used in the case of geography and history. But one thing to be noticed is that every municipal law consists of hundreds of rules, and to memorize that in Article so-and-so certain matters are provided, or that such and such matters are provided in Article so-and-so, is very confusing. To save this confusion the author has provided a very simple and easy method. That is, first, to transform each article number into simple or connected words according to the rules of transformation of numerals; and, secondly, to associate with it the essence of the provided rules.

Example

1. Objects to be Memorized

1 In Section 16, New York Penal Code, the person punishable criminally is defined
2 In Section 96 perjury is defined
3 In Section 174 the crime of attempting suicide is provided for.

4. In Section 179 homicide is defined
5. In Section 224 robbery is defined
6. In Section 686 the penalty for attempt to commit a crime is specified.

2 Association

1 (16—person punishable)	Failure in *business* does not make a *person punishable*
2 (96—perjury)	A man of Roman *nose* was convicted of *perjury*
3 (174—attempting suicide)	A man selling a *beautiful puffin* attempted *suicide*
4. (179—homicide)	A man wearing a *beautiful pin* committed *homicide*
5 (224—robbery)	*Thin taffy* was taken by *robber*
6. (686—attempt to commit a crime)	He *attempts* to commit the crime of stealing a *small goose*

§ 4.—Physics, Chemistry, Medical Science, Etc.

In the medical science, for the purpose of memorizing the proportion of the kinds of medicines in compounding, it is most convenient to make the name of the medicine a register. For the purpose of memorizing chemistry,—for instance, the name of the elements, their proportion of associations with each other, and the name of the compound they form,—the name of the element should be associated with its proportion. When there are many elements, first, each element should be associated with each proportion; second, each word formed by an association between the name of the element and its proportion should be again associated, and, thirdly, the name of the compound to be formed by the chemical operation should be associated with it. For the other sciences the reader may infer from what has been explained in the present work the most convenient way by which they can be memorized. Here the detailed explanation is not given, which should not be considered a defect in the work, for the author is quite confident that the reader can easily understand the application of the several methods to them.

APPENDIX.

I. TIME AND METHOD REQUIRED FOR THE STUDY OF THIS SCIENCE.

THERE are two methods of studying mnemonics. One is direct instruction and the other is self-teaching. One of the two methods will naturally require more or less time than the other for the study. From my experience, however, I can state definitely that any one may be able to finish his study in less than thirteen lessons, each lesson consisting of two hours' instruction. Most of the Japanese students did not require more than ten lessons to finish their studies. But here in America, owing to the difference in the language, my explanation cannot be so lucid as it would be in Japanese, and a few additional lessons may be demanded. That is why I said that thirteen lessons will be sufficient. As to self-teaching, I am not safe in making any definite statement about the time, because it depends upon the ability of the student and his diligence in studying the subject. As only about a dozen lessons are demanded in the former case, in the present case none need spend many days over it. Let me give the reader a bit of advice: should he start once in self-teaching, he should never give it up half way. Let him remember that his study means nothing but adapting the natural powers of his brain. Do not feel discouraged with the study because it seems too difficult at first, for its results are amazing in the end.

II. THE PERMANENCE OF THE MEMORY.

There can be no better way to measure the strength of the memory than to make a comparison between the permanence of the scientifically cultivated memory and that of the natural. While it is beyond my power to give exact statistics, because there is a difference wholly or partially dependent upon the capacity of the memorizer and the nature of the things memorized, still I shall set forth some results obtained by myself.

We must bear in mind, however, that the act of repeating is the sole and the absolute method for strengthening the memory-stamp. If, therefore, a thing is once committed to memory, twice, thrice, and over and over again impressed, it will cause the memory-stamp to become surer and surer, and more and more indelible. Even at the moment when the memory-stamp is very nearly effaced, it is apt to revive through the act of repeating. This being true, it is impossible to show a different degree in the measure of the permanence of memory as long as we are not sure of the proportion of repetition between the two memorizers. Suppose we find that two memorizers have used an equal proportion of repeated impressions. Then we have nothing but the sameness of the fixed memory, and the difference between the two methods cannot be inferred. Hence I have ascertained that the memory-stamp which has been repeated after the first memorizing is not to be reckoned in any comparison of the permanence of the memory. According to this assertion, the following results have been obtained by myself.

Degree of the Permanence of Memory.

(1.) In regard to many numbers, characters, vocabularies, and foreign languages, etc, which cannot be remembered as easily as with the aid of mnemonics: In regard to these things there is a great gulf between the scientifically cultivated and the natural memory. For instance, in some cases the cultivated memory may retain impressions for three or four weeks from the time of first memorizing, while the uncultivated memory may be exhausted after two or three days. Again, in other cases the memory-image can be preserved for a week or two by the cultivated memory, but only thirty minutes or an hour by the uncultivated memory; however, in some other cases differences between the two may not occur more than twice or thrice. But in general, when the difficulty of memorizing by the uncultivated memory-power is greater, then the difference is the wider between the permanence of the scientifically cultivated memory and that of the natural. In a word, the scale of difficulty is in an equal ratio with the degree of difference in the permanence of the two.

(2.) In regard to things which present less difficulty in memorizing, either for the cultivated memory or for the natural, on account of the easy nature of things and facts, we have very little to say, except that there is a difference between the permanence of the scientifically cultivated memory and that of the natural in some small degree; that is to say, the former is comparatively firm and unyielding, therefore preferable.

III FORGETFULNESS.

Will the memory-image obtained through the system of mnemonics never be forgotten? This question has been put to me from time to time. But let me state here at once that it has no valuable scientific application. Our daily experience teaches us that it is natural for us to lose many a memory-image as the days go by. Therefore it will make no difference about its being forgotten, whether it has been obtained through mnemonics or not, should the forgetting take place prior to the growing up of a fixed memory-image. To memorize is active, and to forget is passive; both actions are natural to man. But to repress forgetfulness we have a simple, easy, yet effective method. This is the act of repeating, with repetition again and again at the proper time,—that is, while the memory-image is not yet obliterated: it will grow into the never-to-be-forgotten, and will be comprised in the family of the fixed memories.

IV THE BENEFIT OF MNEMONICS.

There can be no doubt that when we memorize things by a scientific method, we shall have far greater advantages than when we act with the mere aid of the natural uncultivated memory-power. The first great benefit is that we economize our time, and the second, that we economize our brain-power.

1. The Economy of our Time.

In order to discuss this subject in an accurate manner, we must divide it into two parts, as in the previous discussion of the permanence of the memory. But, as we have seen, the second part of it is not so important as the first. Here we shall simply follow the first, omitting the second, in considering the economy of our time. The degree, greater or less, of the economy of time depends upon the capacity of the memorizer and upon the nature of the things which are to be memorized. For instance, by the scientific method one can memorize at once such things as many numbers, vocabularies, foreign languages, etc , in ten or fifteen minutes. On the other hand, it will take the natural memorizer two or three hours. There are some other things which may be committed to memory by the scientific memorizer in an hour or two, while the same things will take the natural memorizer ten or fifteen hours. On the whole, counting the least advantage in every comparison, the scientific memorizer spends no more than one-third of the time required by the natural memorizer.

2 The Economy of Brain-Power.

I am well aware that people have been greatly interested in this timely subject. At the same time, I am aware that they are apt to misunderstand its real value and character. Here is my declaration: the economy of our brain-power surpasses that of our time.

Now, men may very likely imagine that though mnemonics may serve for the economy of time in memorizing, yet, *per contra*, it will waste more of the brain-power on account of the saving of time. To illustrate: here is a certain object which may be supposed to be memorized by the natural memorizer within say ten hours and with a hundredth part of the brain-power, and the same memorized by the scientific memorizer in only an hour. Here they jump at the conclusion that in the last case a hundredth part of the brain-power is spent in an hour. This inference may seem fair at first, but is very erroneous after all. As we all know, after allowing our brain-power to battle for itself, without compass or method, against complicated things and facts, we feel that it is greatly exhausted. On the other hand, leading our brain-power systematically to uncomplicated things and facts, we shall feel less exhausted by our brain-work. So it is with our memory work. Our memory-power without scientific aid always struggles with difficulty against things and facts, while if we direct our memory-power scientifically we can work effectually and, I may add, cheerfully. Let me illustrate a little further: you who apply the methods of mnemonics in order to memorize things may be likened to those who travel on the wheel or by the train, instead of on foot, and your brain-power is less wasted, or more economized, than it otherwise would be.

INDEX.

	PAGE
Accompaniment mode	34
Adding transformation	24
Analogous sound in mode of association	33
in transformation	25
Analogy mode	33
Analysis of linked ideas	63, 65, 70
of registered ideas	54, 57, 58, 60
Application of composing method	79
of linking method	63
of methods in regard to special objects	90
of mnemonics to the study of sciences	165
of registering method	52
Association	31
Attributing mode	37
Benefit of mnemonics	174
Causation mode	34
Changing transformation	24
Combined application of the three methods	86
of composing and linking methods	84
of linking and registering methods	74
Composing method	78
mode	37
transformation	28
Condition required for the mental register	43
Connected words	20
in application of composing method	80
in that of linking method	64
in that of registering method	59
in memorizing unfamiliar things and events	154–156
in transformation of numerals	98–101, 103, 104
Connection of unfamiliar things and events with their names	162

INDEX.

	PAGE
Construction of mental register	43
Contiguity mode	36
Contrary mode	33
Definition of mnemonics	13
Demonstration mode	36
Denoting mode	32
Difference between the composing and linking methods	82
between the linking and registering methods	73
Disconnected words	21
in application of composing method	80
in that of linking method	65
in that of registering method	60
in transformation of numerals	105, 106
Dividing transformation	27
Establishment of the registering method	42
Exercise in memorizing names	147
in memorizing numerals	116
in memorizing poetical compositions	142
in memorizing sentences and speeches	133
Explanation of composing method	78
of linking method	61
of registering method	42
Foreign languages, for memorizing	123
Forgetfulness	173
Form of associating ideas	39
Fundamental processes	22
General application of methods	42
General discussion	13
Geography	165
History	167
Identical sound in mode of association	32
in transformation	25
Identity mode	32
Imagining mode	37
Kinds of mental register	44
of unknown things and events	150
Law, application of mnemonics to	168
Linking method	61
Literal transformation	24
Locality mode	34

INDEX.

	PAGE
Memorizing foreign languages	123
names	147
numerals	91
poetical composition	142
sentences and speeches	133
unknown things and events	150
Memory objects	19
Mental register	43
Methods	40
composing	78
for studying this science	171
linking	61
registering	42
Modes of association	32
attributing	37
composing	37
denoting	32
imagining	37
Names, for memorizing	147
Natural memory	13
Numbers	20, 21
Numerals for memorizing	90
Numeration for transformation	108
Order of the words taken to form an association of ideas	38
Origin of representing characters of numerals	91
of the special rules for transformation of foreign languages	125
of those of numeration	109
Permanence of the memory	172
Precedent word in association	38
Principles	14
Register	44
Registering method	42
Relation of disconnected words to linking method	65
Removing transformation	24
Repetition of register	51
Representation by analogy	151
by attributing	151
by identification	151
by position	151
by selection	150

INDEX.

	PAGE
Representing transformation	27
Selection and concentration	157
Simple words	20
in application of composing method	79
in that of linking method	63
in that of registering method	53
in transformation of numerals	91, 94, 95, 111, 11
Special objects in application of methods	90
rules for transforming foreign languages	123
unfamiliar things and events	150
Specification mode	34
Speeches, for memorizing	133
Subsequent word in association	38
Things and facts or events	19
as register	45, 50
Time and method required for the study of this science	171
Time mode	35
Transformation	23
by analogous sounds	25
by identical sounds	25
composing	28
dividing	27
literal	24
of disconnected words	68
of foreign languages	123, 127
of numerals	90
of numeration	108
of unknown things and events	152
representing	27
Unknown things and events for memorizing	150
Words	20
connected	20
disconnected	21
for register	45, 50
simple	20

COMMENDATORY EXPRESSIONS.

Letter from Prince Atsumaro Konoye, President of the Japanese House of Lords and of the Japanese Nobles' College.

July 21, 1895.

MR KIKUJIRO WADAMORI:

MY DEAR SIR,—Many thanks for your kindness in giving the lectures and experiments on the subject of mnemonics in the Nobles' College and Kogo Club. Your new theories are a great discovery, and of such wonderful practical bearing as to excite great interest. It is my desire to help you in every possible way towards the publication of your system

Hoping to have an opportunity of expressing my sentiments to you in person, and that you will meanwhile accept this as a partial evidence of my gratitude for your kindness, I remain,

Yours very truly,

PRINCE ATSUMARO KONOYE.

Letter from Mr. Jigoro Kano, President of the High Normal College in Tokio.

July 7, 1895.

MR. KIKUJIRO WADAMORI

DEAR SIR,—We thank you for your kindness in having come to our college and given a lecture with experiments on the subject of mnemonics. We congratulate you on the success of your valuable work after the hard study of several years. Hereby we desire to express our best thanks

　　　　　　　Yours very respectfully,

　　　　　　　　　　　JIGORO KANO, PH.D.,
　　　　　　　　　　　President of High Normal College

Letter from the Professors of the Tokio Imperial University.

　　　　　　　　　　　　　TOKIO, June 23, 1895.

MR KIKUJIRO WADAMORI:

DEAR SIR,—We thank you for being so kind as to teach your new laws of mnemonics in such manner as to enable us to apply them. After the lecture and a little practice, we are able to memorize many words, phrases, and numerals without any trouble. With more practice in applying the laws, they will doubtless help not a little in every branch of scientific investigation. As your lectures are now closed, we take the present opportunity of offering our thanks

　　　　　　Yours very truly,

　　　　　　　　　MUNEO KUMAKAWA, M.D,
　　　　　　　　　　　Professor, Medical Department.
　　　　　　　　　ASATARO OKADA, D.C L,
　　　　　　　　　　　Professor, Law Department.
　　　　　　　　　KENJI TSURUTA, D Sc.,
　　　　　　　　　　　Professor, Department of Physics.
　　　　　　　　　AIKICHI TANAKADATE, D Sc,
　　　　　　　　　　　Professor, Department of Physics.
　　　　　　　　　HIROSHI TANAKA, B V.M.,
　　　　　　　　　　　Professor, Agricultural Department.
　　　　　　　　　SAKURO TANABE, D.Sc,
　　　　　　　　　　　Professor, Engineering Department.
　　　　　　　　　JINTARO TAKAHASHI, M D.,
　　　　　　　　　　　Professor, Medical Department.

From Mr. Eiichi Shibusawa, President of Tokio Chamber of Commerce and of the First National Bank in Tokio, etc.

Mr. Kikujiro Wadamori, upon completion of his work, asked me to add a word. In the spring of this year I heard his lecture on new laws of memory, with experiments, and was greatly astonished at the scientific results. Then I said to myself· "It is, however, an art special to the author himself, and of no avail to the public." On my expressing that opinion, he assured me it was entirely erroneous. I then tried to study his laws with several gentlemen, and to our great surprise we found them to be established on such basis as made them capable of being put in practice by any learner Consequently I persuaded him to publish them and set forth their great advantages to the public In that way was originated the present work

When I once read in Chinese history the story of Cho-Jin, in the time of the "Tang" dynasty, whose memory was so retentive that he never needed to look at a book twice, I thought it a foolish exaggeration Now upon learning the author's laws of memorizing, I have ascertained that history has not deceived us I earnestly hope that each seeker after knowledge may learn the author's laws, and so apply them for memorizing as to be like the ancient Cho-Jin.

EIICHI SHIBUSAWA.

TOKIO, July 28, 1895.

DEC 15 1898
FEB 3 1899

Lightning Source UK Ltd.
Milton Keynes UK
UKHW020640120521
383587UK00005B/220